THE
FUNERAL
BOOK
FOR
HOMILISTS
AND
PRESIDERS

edited by

ELTIN GRIFFIN, O. CARM.

TWENTY-THIRD PUBLICATIONS
BAYARD 🌀 Mystic, CT 06355

Second printing 2001

Revised, North American Edition 2000.

Originally published as *The Funeral Book* by Columba Press,
Dublin, Ireland in 1998.

Twenty-Third Publications
A Division of Bayard
185 Willow Street
P.O. Box 180
Mystic, CT 06355
(860) 536-2611
(800) 321-0411

ISBN:1-58595-013-0
Library of Congress Catalog Card Number: 99-76893
Printed in the U.S.A.

CONTENTS

THE FUNERAL BOOK
FOR HOMILISTS AND PRESIDERS

PREFACE

Quite a slice of my life as a priest has gone into funeral ministry, from the old days when the ritual was virtually all in Latin, except for the prayers and gospel reading at the graveside, to the now more fully developed rites in the vernacular.

One has witnessed enormous change for the better. The specimen homilies in this book are in response to repeated requests. One hopes that would-be homilists will take advantage of the larger scenario provided here, the lengthy commentary on the funeral rites, the possibilities for evangelization both in preaching and in the conduct of the ritual itself, sensitivity in the choice of readings for the funerals of particular individuals, and the topic of the month of November, with its fresh and exciting approach to eschatology.

We bring more than the externals of the rite to funeral celebrations. We bring ourselves, together with our assimilation of the Word of God and of the underlying theology of the rite. We bring sensitivity, a sense of prayer and compassion. Even though we are celebrating death, paradoxically, we can bring faith alive.

Eltin Griffin, O. Carm.

Part One

PASTORAL PRACTICE

MAKING THE MOST OF THE ORDER OF CHRISTIAN FUNERALS

Thomas R. Whelan, C.S.Sp.

Why Funeral Rites?

Death is an everyday occurrence, and yet something inside us refuses to acknowledge it as "normal." When a relative or friend dies, we experience much more than grief due to a mere physical separation. The very question of *our own* mortality raises its head, and we find this difficult to deal with because it presents issues that touch us at the very core of our existence. Yet, we know that everyone who is born must die. There is a helplessness associated with death and dying, and we can only deal with this properly in the context of a wider horizon of meaning if we are to be rescued from despair. The rituals we employ at the time of the death and burial of a loved one serve to help us come to terms with a painful loss. They also attempt to offer meaning when all else seems to have failed.

Funerals: Rituals Surrounding Death

Funeral rites represent one of the most ancient and universal cultural forms in existence today. The rites that accompany and follow death serve a number of purposes that seem to go beyond any particular culture. They address basic human requirements in times of bereavement. Rituals surrounding death

- respond to a desire to pray for and accompany the deceased to his or her final resting place;
- create an "environment" whereby those who mourn can be taken care of—in particular, through the offer of consolation and the reassurance of others;
- propose a context of hope, and a gentle but firm support. Mourners, and the wider community to which the deceased belonged, need to readjust their lives. Life from now on will be without their loved one.

Funeral rites, in any culture or belief system, are about much more than simple burial services. They help mark the stages of a painful journey and lead the bereaved to a new chapter in their lives.

Deeper reflection leads us to the realization that the rites used must be capable of bearing the weight of the mystery of death. For a Christian, this mystery carries the added dimension of being understood in the context of Christ's death and resurrection. We quickly think also of the deceased's participation in the Easter mystery of Christ through baptism (see Rom 6:3–5). Furthermore, whatever rites we use must be capable of helping mourners address their own fragility in the face of death and the question of the "hereafter" that it raises, as well as their sense of loss and eventual readjustment.

Funerals: Journey with the Bereaved

It may be helpful for a moment to consider funeral rites as representing a type of "rite of passage"—even if we do not wish to take the idea too far. "Rites of passage" refers to a journey that takes place in stages, beginning with a moment of "separation," then moving through an "in-between" or "transition" stage, before arriving at a new "coming together." The *Order of Christian Funerals* is made up of a complexity of rites, and in these some "stages" may be operating at different levels at the same time.

There are many different moments and levels at which "separation" occurs. For some people it can first present itself with the realization that a relative or friend is dying. Another moment of separation happens at the time of death itself (or receiving news of the death). Levels of a realization of "finality" and separation emerge at other points, such as the gathering time with family (when the body has been prepared), or the more decisive closing of the coffin and, later, with burial itself. These different stages of leavetaking need to be suitably marked if mourners are to eventually readjust themselves to life without their beloved one. There needs to be a "closure" before people can move on.[1] Christian funeral practice does this with appropriate prayers and rites.

Funeral rites also serve to lead mourners gently through the "in-between stage" while they are coming to terms with the death of their loved one. This transition stage knows no rules. The normal no longer applies. In fact, the "normal" ceased with the news of the death of a loved one, and will only return—in a new way—when the bereaved come to terms with the trauma that has beset them. It is easy to understand the significance of ritual here. Family and friends may be dealing with many issues brought on by a death. Apart from those already mentioned (the question of mortality, and readjusting to a new situation), other matters sometimes arise. Faith concerns can emerge, maybe tinged with guilt and anger, not least for those for whom the Christian churches bear little relevance. Death throws family members into a new network of relationships that can either reopen wounds or bring about an opportunity for healing. What was "normal" is now open to question. One of the problems of our time is that modern culture attempts to telescope what used to take some time, into a few brief days. Society no longer offers the type of bereavement support it once did. In this respect, Christian funerals are, and ought to be, countercultural. They offer a framework within which gentle support and healing may be found. They play a central part in proposing faith to mourners as a helpful context for dealing with their new reality.

Respecting Ritual and Ritual Moments

The fluid and unsettling nature of this time demands that we give due regard to the rituals that accompany death and burial. Often people have nothing else to hold onto apart from these rites.[2] This is certainly not a time to meddle with them, but rather to show profound respect for the rites themselves and the way they function. One of the many roles of ritual is to offer protection. It can provide a space that is defined by the comfort and security of the "familiar," and within which one can feel safe and slowly regain a sense of "normalcy." Ritual, almost by definition, involves repetition, and this means employing prayers and gestures that are familiar through regular use. Working with the familiar is central to ritual activity—and never more so than during this "transitional" time surrounding the death of a loved one. This point cannot be overemphasized.

Before looking at the *Order of Christian Funerals*, it might be helpful to make a few brief comments on the nature of ritual and its requirements.

- Good ritual places importance on the symbolic. Symbols should be full, generous, simple—and *unexplained.*
- Good ritual involves movement and gesture. Nothing can substitute for the security and comfort of a gentle hug or firm handshake. Accompanying the body to the church and graveside is a gesture of solidarity and support.
- Gesture, like symbol, will reflect abundance and graciousness,

largesse and warmth—without ever being patronizing.

- A well-celebrated liturgy addresses reality through rites and symbols. This has the effect of locating our reality firmly in the context of a greater reality.
- Good ritual places much stock on fullness and on noble simplicity, on authenticity, and on a sense of the mystery that these rites must bear.

Symbol and gesture are stronger than word. Certain experiences and moments in life are so traumatic that they are best expressed and responded to through symbol and gesture. When understood, the rites can be celebrated well and fully, and the *liturgy itself* can assume a ministerial role.

Good ritual behavior means that those who lead liturgical prayer must themselves be familiar with the rites. A presider would do well to page through the OCF to see how the various liturgies are structured and how each rite relates to the overall. A presider should also be familiar with the rich *resources* provided in the book. It is helpful to see what each element of the rite (be it gesture, a symbol, or a prayer text) communicates of our Christian belief at this time. A good starting place is the "General Introduction" that prefaces the OCF. It is a relatively short but excellent text. It reflects an enormous degree of pastoral sensitivity and wisdom, gathered over a considerable period of time, from many countries throughout the world.

Order of Christian Funerals: Embodying our Faith

The *Order of Christian Funerals* (OCF) is the resource book of the parish community for its funerals. This book supplies a repertoire of rites, prayers, and readings. It proposes an underlying structure that experience has shown to be most beneficial and supportive for the bereaved. It indicates how a faith climate might be created and sustained—one that would enable the bereaved to mourn fully and regain a sense of equilibrium and meaning. A wise use of the OCF means that ministers will be able to approach funerals with resources appropriate to the pastoral circumstances that present themselves. A knowledge of the "General Introduction," and the introductions that preface each section of the book, will help a pastoral minister find creative ways to communicate to the bereaved a faith-filled understanding of death and journeying. Let us briefly highlight something of the vision that this liturgical ritual reveals.

The first observation to be made is that funeral rites are about more than just burial procedures. They form part of a large pastoral ministry to the sick, the dying, and the bereaved. A local assembly should be prepared to accompany those of its members who are seriously sick. They will do this through their prayer as well as through those individuals who, in various ways, perform a ministry to the sick. Pastoral care will often continue long after the burial so that the bereaved can be accompanied through the "transitional" period until they come to terms with their new situation. The practice of a "Month's Mind" and anniversary Mass—common in some places—contribute to this process of re-integration.

A second point to note is the vision of "church" found in the OCF. Ministry to the dying and the bereaved is not the preserve of the priest. The *full community* has responsibility to offer a faith-filled support. This can take many forms. Obviously a community that has a consciousness of its all-year-round immersion into the mystery of Christ's death and resurrection will be well equipped to offer a faith context for those who are mourning. Specifically, bereavement groups form an important part of an overall ministry. The local assembly should be there to sustain and, often, simply to be with family and close friends, when a loved one is dying or has died.

Baptism supplies the OCF with metaphors and a language with which to speak of death. Reading through the prayers and Scripture texts, one cannot but be struck by the many references and allusions to baptism. We begin our Christian lives with baptism.

Paul described baptism as a death. When initiated, we are plunged into the death of Christ so that we might experience now—if only imperfectly and imperceptibly—resurrection-life in Christ. At our own death, we are brought fully into its completion in Christ.

Another image we meet is that of "eternal life." Again the roots of this are to be found in the initiation sacraments. Baptism immersed us in God's trinitarian life. This is something we are destined to continue when we are called to fullness of life at death, but in a way far greater than anything we could ever perceive. Ministers are encouraged by the OCF to proclaim the victory of life over death.

Walking through the Order of Christian Funerals*

Funeral rites are principally concerned with the final journey that a community makes with its deceased loved one. A task must be accomplished. The dead must be buried. Christian liturgy places a person's death, and the sorrow of the mourners, in the context of Christ's death and our baptismal immersion into that death. We pray for the deceased and allow our faith in the resurrection to sustain those who are bereaved.

The principal ritual unfolds in three moments. Receiving the body at the church is customary in Ireland on the evening before the burial. The central Funeral Liturgy (which normally includes a celebration of the Eucharist) incorporates the Rite of Commendation and Farewell. The procession of journey follows, accompanying the coffin to the place of committal.

Editor's Note for the North American Edition:
The following sections of Fr. Whelan's chapter reflect the Irish context for which they were originally written. In some instances, what he says may not correspond to North American experience. We encourage you to read this section because it offers many fine insights into the practice of our funeral rites. (Citations to the *Order of Christian Funerals* have been changed to the U.S. edition of the rite.) We have also added the chapter on funeral rites in the North American context, especially in the United States, by Fr. Lawrence E. Mick, starting on page 20 of this book.

1. RECEPTION OF THE BODY AT THE CHURCH

After the initial (biblical) greeting of those present, the coffin is sprinkled with blessed water. Where the baptismal fountain is near the door, this might take place as the coffin is brought past, using water from the fountain itself (even if this means taking water from the font into the bucket). In this way the opening words of the prayer, "In the waters of baptism ..." (and subsequent references to baptism), become highlighted by the ritual gesture.

The ritual suggests, for certain occasions, the use of blessed water: on the occasion of gathering in the presence of the body; at the conclusion of a vigil; at the time of the closing of the coffin, where it is described as "a gesture," and at the time of committal. The sprinkling is presumed at the reception in the church, and during the final commendation. The OCF (#36) notes that the use of blessed water primarily evokes a reminder of the deceased's "initiation into the community of faith." The obvious links with baptism can be enhanced when the sprinkling is carried out in an unrushed and generous way, using a traditional sprinkler or an evergreen branch. If circumstances permit, there is no reason why the presider would not place his hand in the font and sprinkle the coffin in a gracious and dignified manner.

A pall, "a sign of the Christian dignity of the person" (#38), may now be placed on the coffin by family members, friends, or the minister (#133). It is done in silence.

Communities for whom the use of the pall is not customary could do well to consider introducing it. It is a large white cloth, of simple design, capable of covering the coffin, and made of good quality cloth. It recalls the baptismal garment put on by the newly baptized, and therefore speaks of quiet and confident hope. As it is a symbol, there should be no designs, texts, or other symbols superimposed on it. It covers the coffin during the liturgy and serves to signify "that all are equal in the eyes of God (see James 2:1–9)" (#38).[3]

The presider leads the way to the central part of the church. An appropriate song is sung during this procession, unless serious pastoral difficulties prevent this (#135). The rite suggests a number of possibilities. If the assembly is not yet accustomed to a fuller music ministry, then a song leader or cantor could lead with some suitable music. A simple antiphon or refrain sung by all to a spoken text is often very effective, and is easy to do.

"Music," says the OCF, "is integral to the funeral rites. It allows the community to express convictions and feelings that words alone may fail to convey. It has the power to console and uplift the mourners and to strengthen the unity of the assembly in faith and love" (#30). Its importance cannot be underestimated.

Whatever music is used, it should "support, console, and uplift the participants and should help to create in them a spirit of hope in Christ's victory over death and in the Christian's share in that victory" (#31). The texts "should express the paschal mystery of the Lord's suffering, death, and triumph over death and should be related to the readings from scripture" (#30).

The choice of music is not guided by a list of the deceased's favorites. Music and text should bear some relation to the mystery of Christ being celebrated.

One further note on music: The practice of "hiring" or importing a soloist for the occasion goes against good taste, and has missed the point about how music functions in relation to the liturgical assembly. An increasing number of communities are developing a music ministry to serve their funeral needs. Parishes can develop a specific ministry of funeral cantor or musician.

After stating principles about music in funerals, the introduction to the OCF pays close attention to the use of Christian symbols in the reception of the body in the church. The Easter candle will have been placed beforehand near where the coffin will rest. A family member, friend, or the presider may now place a symbol of Christian life on the coffin. The OCF supplies possible short texts to accompany this gesture. However, if done gracefully and without haste, with no other action taking place, this can be carried out quite effectively in silence.

A Book of Gospels or a Bible (maybe even that of the deceased) may be carried in procession from the door and placed on the coffin at this time. This gesture underlines the importance of the word of God in the living of Christian life. It also draws attention to the call to be faithful to that word if we wish to be part of God's kingdom (#38).

Alternatively, a cross may be placed on top of the coffin. This symbol highlights the faith statement that we have been called to live our lives by the cross with which we have been marked in baptism. It proclaims the great Christian enigma, that the cross is the way to resurrection and life.

It is good to note OCF #38: "Only Christian symbols may rest on or be placed near the coffin during the funeral liturgy. Any other symbols, for example, national flags, or flags or insignia of associations, have no place in the funeral liturgy." Symbols refer to that which speaks of Christian hope and the person's baptismal life and immersion into Christ's death and resurrection. Personal items associated with the deceased's past life are best used at services apart from the funeral rites. Mass cards can be collected in a basket placed in some convenient location. Wreaths can be arranged somewhere to the side, from where they will be later brought to the place of burial. When either appear on or beside the coffin, they tend to distract from the simplicity, beauty, and directness of the Christian symbols used.

The opening prayer follows. Presiders should be aware of the very large selection of prayers for different circumstances found in the appendix. The OCF notes that the reading of the word of God, which follows, is the high point and central focus of the reception rite (#124). Unless it is impossible to do so, the responsorial psalm should be sung. At the very least, the response itself could be sung by all, with the verses read.

A sense of pastoral responsibility will guide in the choice of appropriate readings. Their purpose is to proclaim the paschal mystery and to offer gentle and hope-filled support to the assembly in its bereavement. The readings present a context for understanding what is happening: a vision of God's kingdom presented by Jesus. The ritual notes that the brief homily that follows is based on the readings, and is not a eulogy (#141). A litany of intercession leads to a suitable concluding prayer and concluding rite.

This liturgy marks an important moment in the journey of farewell to a loved one. Before burial, the community receives the body of the deceased in its place of worship. This is the place where people enter into a new life. They are immersed by baptism into the mystery of Christ's saving death. Here the assembly is nourished in the Eucharist, as was the deceased. The various baptismal symbols, gestures, and images of this liturgy gives expression to a reverence we wish to show toward the body, a temple of God's presence. They also create the context that will inspire the community's funeral prayers as it buries one of its own: a hope informed by faith. Thus enabled, the community offers consolation and support to the family and friends of the deceased. It marks a stage in the process of separation. Normally the rite of reception is not celebrated with Mass, unless this is to be the Funeral Mass.[4]

2. FUNERAL MASS: FINAL COMMENDATION AND FAREWELL

"The funeral Mass is the central liturgical celebration of the Christian community for the deceased" (#128). It is appropriate that the community should gather just one more time in the presence of the deceased, and do what they do together each Sunday—keep the memory of the Lord as they celebrate Eucharist.[5] The Eucharist says all that we want to say about the life-giving death of Christ, into which mystery we were initiated through baptism. It also enables us interpret the death of a deceased person against the death of Christ. It offers us a foretaste of the heavenly banquet to which all are invited. Eucharistic communion unites all the faithful, living and dead, with Christ.

The OCF offers a fine commentary on the Funeral Mass (#128-157), which goes into considerable detail when discussing certain of its elements. There is an obvious desire that this central funeral liturgy would sustain the bereaved at this time of sorrow, and that the mystery of Christ would give reason for their hope. It notes especially that the entrance procession should be accompanied by the singing of a suitable song. What was said above regarding music applies here also. Songs should reflect "profound expression of belief in eternal life and the resurrection" as well as interceding for the deceased (#135). Likewise, the OCF presumes that the responsorial psalm is sung, using one of the many ways in which this can be done. There is no shortage of suitable music resources available. Simple acclamations are easily used during other parts of the liturgy, especially during the eucharistic prayer and communion rite.

Members of the family of the deceased, or friends, may bring to the altar the gifts to be used in the Eucharist. The purpose of this short rite is simply so that the next part of the liturgy can take place. It is not appropriate at this time to carry up symbols of the life of the deceased or personal mementos. To add symbols at this stage is to attempt to make the ritual say something different. A suitable occasion for using personal mementos might well be during a vigil, before or after the reception of the body, or during a brief remembrance of the deceased at the final commendation and farewell.

At the end of the liturgy, the community makes its final farewell to one of its own, whom it now entrusts to the loving mercy of God. The tone changes. We now hear the language of separation and of hope. We recall the invitation extended through Christ, that we enter into his heavenly kingdom. Voice is given in the prayers of our faith, which tells us that we will be reunited, one day, with our deceased sisters and brothers.[6]

This beautiful rite takes place after the prayer after communion (the blessing and dismissal are omitted). It should not be overloaded. It marks the beginning of the final stage of separation, which concludes with burial. The change in emotional intensity at this point is best responded to by ritual simplicity. Extra commentary, explanations, or prayers should not be added to what is already offered. Important, for instance, is the period of silent prayer (#171-2), which takes place after the opening invitation to prayer. Silence is essential here to help in the transition to this final part of the liturgy.

Parish communities with even the most modest means should be able to sing some suitable song of farewell. It is a high point of this rite. This song (along with the prayer and gesture used here) gives expression to the great hope that we will one day be able to join with our deceased sisters and brothers and, with one voice, sing the praises and glory of God. It is a song that gives utterance to a companionship and a communion between heaven and earth, to a sense of urgency in wanting to be in the presence of the Almighty, to a feeling of "going home." If we examine the texts and rite, we see that the final commendation is all about commending the deceased to God, and bidding farewell in prayer and song.

The abundant sprinkling of the coffin with blessed water and profuse incensing—all calmly done—may take place before, during, or after the song of farewell. These gestures give expression to the dignity with which the community upholds the body of the deceased. This person, through baptism, became a living temple of God's presence, and these are signs of farewell. Incense is "a sign of the community's prayers for the deceased rising to the throne of God" (#37). Sufficient incense should be used so that its meaning is self-evident. The prayer of commendation concludes the rite. The final part of the journey to the resting place now begins, and a suitable song or psalm should accompany the procession with the coffin.

3. RITE OF COMMITTAL

The Rite of Committal is simple and direct: short Scripture reading, prayer over the place of burial, committal, intercessions, and, finally, concluding prayer over the people. The rite allows for the sprinkling of the grave and coffin with blessed water and the use of incense, if this is customary. This is practical when a burial takes place at a graveside near to the church. When the place of committal is some distance from the church, a sense of dignity and simplicity suggests that incense and blessed water are not used, unless this can be easily done. The practice of using small plastic bottles of blessed water, hastily sprinkled over coffin and grave, does nothing to express the mystery of baptism, or a respectful Christian farewell.

The custom of scattering some earth on the coffin, where used, ought to be encouraged. It forms an important part of the leave-taking that is being expressed here in a very decisive manner. By making a "closure" here, the road toward healing and the later stages of bereavement is facilitated. It also helps to give ritual poignancy to the prayers, which express, with deep faith, hope in resurrection.

4. RELATED RITES

Among other funeral rites offered by the OCF are:

Prayers after Death—which may be suitably used when the minister makes an initial contact with the family after the death has occurred;

Gathering in the Presence of the Body—a resource that may be found helpful for "when the family first gathers in the presence of the body, when the body is to be prepared for burial, or after it has been prepared" (#109).

Vigil for the Deceased—described as the "principal rite celebrated by the Christian community" between the death and the funeral liturgy. It is ideal, also, for when a wake takes place;

Transfer of the Body to the Church—to be celebrated normally before the closing of the coffin, as family and friends prepare to bring the body of the deceased to the church.

Each rite is preceded by a very short, but excellent, pastoral commentary. Provision is also made for situations in which laypeople will preside and lead the prayer.

Familiarity with these is helpful if they are to be used appropriately and sensitively. The options available should be noted, as well as the rich collections of additional texts found at the back of the ritual book. Each rite, in its own way, marks another stage in the journey. They all belong to an "in-between" stage between receiving the news of the death, the burial, and taking up, once again, normal living. They address situations in which the bereaved must deal with a variety of emotions that may include sorrow, confusion, anger, and emptiness. Prayer leaders should also bear in mind that the mourners present may range from those who are faith-filled believers to those for whom the church bears little relevance. These liturgies ritualize simple gestures (such as the sealing of the coffin and beginning the journey to the church) or necessary happenings (such as making contact with the family immediately after death has taken place, or at the time when the body is prepared for burial). Ritual, in its simplicity and directness, helps articulate the grief and sorrow of those close to the deceased, and quietly offers them the support of the wider church community. The short prayers and verses of Scripture gently remind them of a God who is with them in their pain and confusion. These rites are best celebrated without commentary, explanation, or addition. They are short, but should never be rushed. Their simplicity and directness are best respected.

Other rites are supplied to address occasions when the customary pattern is not followed. There is a rite for the Reception of the Body before the Funeral Mass, used when the funeral liturgy is to take place immediately. The Funeral Liturgy Outside Mass is available for use on those days when a Funeral Mass is not possible (Holy Thursday, Easter Triduum, Sundays of Advent, Lent, and Easter), and when pastoral or other circumstances suggest this to be the best option. Part II of the ritual presents Funeral Rites for Children. An appendix gives the Rite of Committal at a Crematorium.

5. LITURGICAL MINISTRY

A useful context for understanding how liturgical ministry is best exercised is indicated by the realization that it is the church that gathers to mourn the death of one of its own. It is therefore the church community that supplies ministers on such occasions. Given the fact that most funerals take place on weekdays, some parishes have a group of ministers who offer their services for funerals, so that the liturgy might be celebrated with the care it deserves. Appropriate liturgical ministries include those common in any parish: readers, musicians, hospitality, and special ministers of the Eucharist, as well as pallbearers.

If ministers of hospitality are available, they can contribute greatly to putting mourners at ease as they arrive, especially those who may not be familiar with Catholic practices, or who are not regular churchgoers. Consideration needs to be given to the ministry of reader. Should family members be the principal or even sole source for liturgical ministry? A balance needs to be kept between enabling members to participate in this ministry, and having readings badly proclaimed by people who are not accustomed to reading in liturgy, or who may find themselves unable to read properly due to their grief. Other opportunities for encouraging family members and friends of the deceased to participate actively include the placing of the pall on the coffin at the reception of remains, the placing of Christian symbols on the coffin (if this is being done), and leading the prayers of intercession. They should be encouraged to take as active a part as circumstances and their grief allow. It is interesting that with regard to musicians, the OCF #153 considers a cantor and an organist (or other instrumentalists) as normative. They serve to assist the assembly in singing the relevant parts. A choir is considered optional.

Conclusion

The *Order of Christian Funerals* is the resource book for the Christian rites that surround the death of a believer. Careful use of and selection from a repertoire of rites and Christian symbols assist those who mourn to readjust themselves to the human loss they experience. It helps support them in their pain by its calm and faith-filled assurance of the resurrection of Christ and all that this means. The Easter mystery of Christ transforms, and offers, not just hope, but a context for understanding all death. The OCF concerns itself principally with the central ritual moments that lead the family and assembly on the journey of farewell from home or hospital, to church, and to grave. A wider bereavement ministry will assist the mourners on their continuing journey. Local custom will suggest the importance to be attached to the Month's Mind and first anniversary Mass, which also form part of the community's ministry to the bereaved as they go through their final stages of readjustment.

The funeral rites will at all times gently and comfortingly allow Christian hope and faith to inform the way it supports and journeys with its mourners, that they may come to terms with the reality that has invaded their lives. When circumstances permit, the family and friends of a deceased person can grow into a deep awareness and appreciation of how the paschal mystery of Christ, into which we were all immersed through baptism, can enrich our understanding of God's plan.

NOTES

1. Placing a board with artificial grass over the grave rather than throwing earth on the coffin (as is the custom in some local places), can delay or deny a final separation. One could well ask, to what extent does this make both the social and psychological transition to the next stage of bereavement more difficult?

2. It is important to acknowledge the meaning that ritual can have at moments like this, even to those who rarely, if ever, go to church.

3. "For this reason, any national flag or the flags or insignia of associations to which the deceased belonged are to be *removed* from the coffin at the entrance of the church. They may be replaced after the coffin has been taken from the church" (#132). Dennis C. Smolarski notes that "The ritual adds the words 'even Christian associations' and even includes the phrase 'or symbols of ministry.' These specifications in the Canadian edition try to emphasize that those things that distinguish people during life—military service, membership in Catholic fraternal organizations, even ordained ministers within the church—must not distinguish the dead, who are equal before God" (*Sacred Mysteries: Sacramental Principles and Liturgical Practice* [New York/ Mahwah, NJ: Paulist Press, 1995] 145).

4. When the reception of the body takes place before the Funeral Mass, the relevant section of the OCF is followed. The rite follows the same pattern as outlined above up to the placing of Christian symbols on the coffin. The presider then makes the customary reverence of the altar, using incense if appropriate, and then beginning the opening prayer of Mass. It should be noted that the normal introductory rites of Mass are omitted: sign of cross, greeting, and penitential rite.

5. When the Funeral Mass must take place on a Sunday, pastoral sensitivity will help choose between retaining all or some of the readings and prayers proper to the Sunday, or using those of the funeral liturgy. It is never appropriate to use funeral texts and readings on Sundays of Advent, Lent and Easter, or on solemnities of obligation. The readings on these occasions, however, provide a wonderful context for speaking about the death of a Christian.

6. The final commendation and farewell is always used, be it as a conclusion of the Funeral Mass or other liturgy, or at the cemetery.

CELEBRATING FUNERALS IN THE UNITED STATES

Lawrence E. Mick

A Challenge for Planning

One of the most difficult challenges for liturgy planners and presiders is creating good worship for funerals. There are several factors that account for the difficulty of the challenge. The most obvious is the limitation of time. All the other liturgies we celebrate can be, and usually are, scheduled well in advance. But death seldom gives us much warning.

Of course, some people who have a terminal illness do have the wisdom to plan their own funeral rites. This is often a very powerful experience of shared faith and love when the planning is shared with family members and friends. It also offers a final gift from the dying person to those left behind, because they will not have the burden of making so many decisions once death has occurred.

But even when detailed plans have been made, it is still

uncertain just when death will come, and thus there is still pressure caused by the limited time available for preparations between death and the funeral rites. Arranging for servers, musicians, choir, ushers, lectors, communion ministers, prayer leaders, meal coordinators, and other ministries in a day or two is never easy.

Another reason that planning is difficult is that family members, who should be involved in the process and have the right to make a number of decisions, are frequently quite unprepared to even consider such issues. There is so much to be done that the temptation is to ask the pastor or the bereavement committee to make all the decisions about the readings and music and rituals. Most Catholics have had little or no experience preparing liturgical services, so they feel inadequate and ill-at-ease when asked to take part in such planning during a time of great stress and sorrow.

Moreover, in our culture there is a strong tendency to deny the reality of death and its inevitability. We really prefer not to talk about it or even think about it until we have to do so. This means that many Catholics have never considered what they would prefer for their own funeral or for their loved ones. Even when death is the culmination of a long illness, many people have given absolutely no thought in advance to the funeral rituals and the decisions required to make them good celebrations.

Another dimension of the challenge of funeral rites is dealing with Catholics who have not been active for many years. Sometimes the deceased was inactive, and more often many of the family members are inactive. Despite their absence from church worship at other times, when death comes most people expect the church to be there for them and to minister to them. It always takes sensitive pastoral care to deal with people at the time of death, but it requires even more care when they have not been connected to the Christian community on an ongoing basis.

When such people have been inactive for a long time, there is sometimes a problem, too, with the memories they have of Catholic funerals before the recent reforms. Images of black vestments and the *Dies Irae* may be dominant in shaping their ideas and attitudes about the funeral. Of course, this is also sometimes true for active Catholics, especially if they have not participated in many funerals in recent years.

Even when the deceased and the family have been active, it is almost a certainty that non-members will be part of the rituals. This is true of most funeral Masses and graveside services and even more likely for services at the funeral home. Funeral planning must always be aware of ecumenical issues and strive to find ways to allow everyone present to participate in whatever degree is appropriate.

The Structure of the Rite

Another common obstacle to good planning is a lack of familiarity with the various rituals that are part of the funeral rite. This is common on the part of families and sometimes even on the part of planners and other ministers. Bereavement committees and all who are involved in funeral ministry need a thorough understanding of the various rituals and the different ways in which they may be combined to meet the needs of particular situations.

The *Order of Christian Funerals* contains six different rituals, three major and three minor. The major ones are the Vigil, the Funeral Liturgy, and the Rite of Committal. The minor ones are Prayers after Death, Gathering in the Presence of the Body, and the Transfer of the Body to the Church or to the Place of Committal. Not all of these are used with every funeral, though the major rituals are employed for most.

The earlier edition of this ritual spoke of different "stations" during the funeral rites, which was one way of reminding us that we need to view the process as a whole. It is a journey taken by the deceased and the mourners that has several "stops" along the way where different rituals are celebrated. It is important to see the differing emphases this journey has at different points.

Immediately after death or perhaps when the parish ministers first meet with the family, the Prayers after Death offer a simple service that draws the family together in prayer. When the family gathers for the beginning of visitation at the funeral home (or sometimes in the church), the service for Gathering in the Presence of the Body can be a welcome structure in which to express the family's feelings and concerns at a frequently difficult moment.

The Vigil for the Deceased (also called the Wake Service in the earlier edition) provides a fuller opportunity for prayer with the family and with friends who have come to the visitation. The Rite for the Transfer of the Body to the Church or to the Place of Committal is ideal for a time of prayer just before the body is carried from the funeral home to the church for the Funeral Liturgy. If there is no church service for some reason, it can also be used before the body is taken to the place of committal.

The Funeral Liturgy is normally the core of the funeral rites. It may either be a Funeral Mass or a Funeral Liturgy Outside Mass, which is primarily a Liturgy of the Word. In both cases, it is framed by the reception of the body at the entrance to the church (unless the visitation was held at church, in which case the reception precedes the Vigil Service) and the final commendation before the body is taken to the place of committal. The final ritual included in the funeral rites is the Rite of Committal celebrated at the graveside or at the crematorium.

If the body has already been cremated before the Funeral Liturgy, an indult for the United States granted by the Congregation for Divine Worship and the Discipline of the Sacraments allows the presence of the cremated remains during the liturgy. These are to be in a "worthy vessel" and are placed on a small table or stand where the coffin is usually placed. The remains may be carried to this spot in the entrance procession or be put in place beforehand. Prayers that do not refer to honoring or burying the body should be chosen, and a few alternate texts are provided in the 1997 appendix to the *Order of Christian Funerals*. The Rite of Committal is then celebrated at the cemetery or columbarium as soon as possible after the Funeral Liturgy.

Each of these rituals requires preparation and pastoral judgments. Pastoral ministers must decide which of the rituals to use and which options within each best meet the needs of the family and friends of the deceased. The danger is the temptation to settle into one unvarying routine that is applied to every funeral the parish celebrates. Such a routine makes things easier on the ministers, but it seldom offers all the pastoral care that the church should offer to its people when they encounter death.

This is a moment of great importance to every human being, whether they are active Catholics or inactive, Christians of another denomination or non-Christians, believers or agnostics or atheists. Death confronts every human being with questions of the meaning and purpose of life and the possibility of life beyond the grave. Because it raises such deep issues, it is always a difficult time and requires much sensitivity on the part of the church's ministers. Creating a pastoral practice that truly meets the needs of the bereaved—with the multiplicity of circumstances and personalities involved—takes a deep commitment and much effort. To short-circuit this process is to miss a powerful opportunity to preach God's word and manifest God's love to people who are more than usually open to both.

Bereavement Committees
Many parishes have discovered the great value of having a group of people devoted to ministry to the dying and the bereaved. The

Order of Christian Funerals reminds us that "the responsibility for the ministry of consolation rests with the believing community" (#9). The death of a member of the community calls the whole community to respond in a variety of ways, offering prayers, sympathy, and practical support to the family and especially by gathering for the celebration of the funeral rites.

Within every parish, however, there are those who have a special ability to manifest the care and concern of the church in the face of death. A bereavement committee composed of such members is invaluable in any parish, especially as the number of priests continues to decline.

Some on the committee will attend to the myriad practical details, thus freeing the family to concentrate on planning the funeral and giving them time for prayer. They may provide meals for the family, house-sit while the family is at the funeral home and at the church, arrange for a meal after the funeral, either at the parish or at the family home, and provide baby-sitting during the visitation or funeral.

Others will focus primarily on preparing the different liturgical moments of these days. They meet with the family to find out their preferences among the readings and music available for the Vigil Service, the Funeral Liturgy, and the Rite of Committal. They contact the musician(s) and the funeral choir. They might arrange for the ministers needed at the liturgies, such as ushers, servers, lectors, and communion ministers. Often they also communicate to the preacher whatever they can learn about the deceased and the family, especially if the family is not known to the preacher.

Some on the committee might take the responsibility for leading one or more of the various rituals that make up the funeral rites. The Prayers after Death, the rite for Gathering in the Presence of the Body, and the rite for the Transfer of the Body might be led by members of the committee more often than by the priest or deacon. Even the Vigil Service and the Rite of Committal may be conducted by a committee member. This is becoming more common as the number of priests dwindles, especially in larger parishes that may have more than one funeral on a given day.

Still others on the committee might focus on follow-up. One of the most neglected aspects of pastoral ministry to the bereaved is contact in the days and weeks following the funeral. During the hectic days between death and burial, there is constant activity and a steady stream of visitors. Often after the funeral, however, the bereaved are left alone, both by friends and by the parish. Continuing contact by parish members can be a vital ministry in helping the bereaved adjust to their changed life after the death of a loved one. This is especially important when the deceased leaves a spouse or other caretaker who now must adjust to living alone.

A Funeral Choir

Many parishes have been blessed with the formation of a funeral choir, composed usually of parishioners who are retired or self-employed or who work at home and are thus free to come for most funeral liturgies. Such a choir provides a wonderful ministry to the family by supporting their singing during the liturgy and lending a sense of beauty to the worship. Their presence is also a gift in itself, especially when the gathered family and friends are few in number. The liturgy always needs a community of faith. While the Order of Christian Funerals reminds us that this is a responsibility of the whole believing community, in practice it is often the choir that makes the community present.

It should be noted that the Order of Christian Funerals also calls for music to be part of the Vigil Service, the Rite of Committal, and the procession if that is possible. Parishes should consider seriously the value of music at these times, perhaps especially at the Vigil Service and at the graveside. The assumption that it is impossible because there are no instruments or professional musicians present neglects the church's long tradition of unaccompanied singing. A good cantor can easily lead the mourners in a responsorial psalm during the Vigil Service or at the grave. An opening song for the Vigil Service, carefully chosen from among those likely to be widely known, can do much to move the gathering into a true sense of worship and prayer. In a similar way, an opening or closing song for the Rite of Committal does much to create a sense of dignity and prayer in that outdoor situation. If you have a funeral choir, consider whether a few of those singers might be trained as cantors or song leaders to provide music for these other moments in the funeral rites.

Stages on a Journey

The rites provided in the *Order of Christian Funerals* envision three major ritual moments: the Vigil Service, the Funeral Liturgy (either Mass or a Funeral Outside of Mass), and the Rite of Committal at the cemetery or crematorium.

The first step in understanding these rites is to recognize that there is a progression implied in them. They are three stages in the journey that the mourners make with the support of the parish community. Paying attention to the different purposes of these three ritual moments will enable planners to provide pastorally effective (as well as liturgically proper) worship experiences.

The Vigil Service is the first major ritual that is offered to the mourners. The family and friends of the deceased need an opportunity to grieve, to acknowledge their loss as they remember the life of the one they loved. At this first stage of the journey, it is not reasonable to expect everyone to be able to focus strongly on the resurrection and to celebrate the paschal mystery. At the same time, what the church offers the mourners as help to deal with their grief is precisely a word of hope that is based on the death and resurrection of Jesus Christ. The challenge is to speak that word in a way that is clearly respectful of the loss and pain the mourners are experiencing.

The Funeral Liturgy, as the second stage on the journey, is intended to focus more strongly on the promise of resurrection that is implicit in the celebration of the Eucharist. Even if the Funeral Liturgy Outside of Mass is used, the emphasis is still on the paschal mystery. The one who has died is seen as vitally linked to Christ, whose death led to resurrection. This primal truth of our faith is the basis of the whole panoply of the funeral rites, but in the Funeral Liturgy properly speaking, it is highlighted as the basis for celebration. Even in the face of death Christians gather to give thanks and praise to God for all that was accomplished through Christ Jesus for our salvation.

The Rite of Committal at the cemetery or at the crematorium is a rite designed to provide closure to this initial journey of grief. Grieving will continue, of course, for weeks and years and maybe a lifetime, but this initial and public phase comes to closure as the body of the loved one is entrusted to the earth or committed to the flames.

The Vigil Service

Older Catholics will remember when the prayers at the funeral home consisted of the rosary, led by the priest or a lay leader. This custom offered great comfort to many, and it may be pastorally appropriate to include a public recitation of the rosary at some point during the visitation.

This does not mean that the rosary should substitute for the Vigil Service that is part of the *Order of Christian Funerals.* The Vigil Service is part of the official Catholic ritual for the burial of a member of the church. It offers the word of God to those who mourn along with prayers and songs that encourage and sustain their faith.

Since at least some of those present at the visitation when the service is celebrated will not be Catholics, this ritual offers a better opportunity for all to participate in prayer than the uniquely

Catholic custom of the rosary. Designing a service that will foster the participation of all should be a constant concern as the Vigil Service is prepared.

Planning the Vigil Service is often easier than executing the plan. It is often difficult even to get everyone's attention in the midst of the visitation, and many of those who are present at that moment may not be expecting a service of prayer.

One of the most effective ways to signal the beginning of this time of prayer might be with music. The *Order of Christian Funerals* clearly expects singing to be part of this rite: "Music is integral to any vigil, especially the vigil for the deceased. In the difficult circumstances following death, well-chosen music can touch the mourners and others present at levels of human need that words alone often fail to reach" (#68). This expectation in the rite should not be taken lightly. If a musician can be present, it will lend a strong note of both solemnity and beauty to the ritual. Many funeral homes have a piano or small organ available; a guitarist or other instrumentalist (a single flute, for example) also can be a great help in supporting the singing.

If an instrumentalist is not available, a song leader or cantor can lead the singing. Such a person might even provide the signal for prayer by singing a single verse of the opening song for the service. Then when the attention of all has been gained, the presider can urge everyone to join in the service, begin with the greeting, and then invite all to sing the song they just heard. Providing a simple song sheet is obviously helpful; remember to get copyright permission. Picking a well-known hymn common to several Christian traditions will help facilitate the participation of all present.

After the song the introductory rites conclude with an invitation to prayer and the opening prayer. A liturgy of the word follows, with two readings separated by a psalm, which also should be sung. If the parish has learned that responsorial psalms are always a sung part of the liturgy, this pattern will be familiar to parish members who are present. If no one is available who can sing the entire psalm, consider at least singing a simple refrain between spoken verses.

The texts for the opening song, the readings, and the psalm should be chosen after the texts are selected for the Funeral Liturgy. This is not only to avoid duplication, but to choose texts that reflect the flow of the funeral rites. The readings for the Vigil might be chosen because they support the need to grieve and recognize the sorrow of the mourners. Then the readings at church can move more strongly toward the proclamation of the paschal mystery and the promise of resurrection. The music might be selected according to the same principles.

A brief homily concludes the liturgy of the word. Like the homily at church, this is not intended to be a eulogy of the deceased but a proclamation of the faith of the church. It should flow from the readings chosen, but in general it might focus on the love and mercy of God as a comfort and a reason for hope in the midst of the pain of loss.

The third part of the rite consists of prayers of intercession, with several petitions concluded by the Lord's Prayer and a concluding oration. The rite notes that, after these prayers, "a member or friend of the family may speak in remembrance of the deceased." This seems a much better time for this kind of reminiscence than during the liturgy at church. The Vigil concludes with a blessing and perhaps a final song.

Another option for the Vigil Service is to use Evening Prayer (or Morning Prayer if the visitation is in the morning) from the Office for the Dead. As parishes gradually recover the tradition of the Liturgy of the Hours as part of parish life, this might be an ideal choice for the Vigil in many cases. Part IV of the *Order of Christian Funerals* offers guidance and texts for this option.

One of the challenges for celebrating a worthy Vigil is to gather members of the parish at that time. It might be best to standardize the time for such a service, at least insofar as visitation hours allow. A phone chain among the bereavement committee and other parish organizations might be another way to let parishioners know the ideal time to come for visitation. The Vigil Service is the parish's primary moment to offer comfort and support during the visitation.

The Funeral Liturgy

The *Order of Christian Funerals* uses the term "Funeral Liturgy" instead of "Funeral Mass" in recognition of the fact that sometimes it may not be possible to have the Eucharist, especially as the number of priests continues to decline. Even when a priest is available, pastoral judgment might suggest having the Funeral Liturgy Outside of Mass on some occasions; if all or most of those who will gather for the service are not Catholic, it might be better to conduct a service in which all can participate rather than try to celebrate Eucharist with those who cannot share in the meal (see #178-3). It may also be necessary to use this service on the few days of the year when the Funeral Mass is prohibited: holydays of obligation, Holy Thursday, and the Triduum (#178-1).

Nevertheless, there is a profound appropriateness to the celebration of the Eucharist when a member of the church dies, for the Eucharist is our fullest celebration of the death and resurrection of Christ. The death of a Christian is linked to the death of Christ, a death once shared in symbol in baptism and now shared in the reality of human death. And, as Paul tells us, "if we have grown into union with him through a death like his, we shall also be united with him in the resurrection" (Rom 6:5).

The main challenge of the Funeral Liturgy is to make it a real celebration. Many funerals take place with only a handful of people, and many of them participate minimally. The family is seated in a few rows near the front, while other friends are scattered about the rest of the church. There is little sense of the community of faith or of the support that those grieving need from their brothers and sisters in Christ.

One obvious step to improve this situation would be to schedule funerals when people are free to come, i.e., in the evening rather than on a weekday morning. Some families have embraced this option, but it is still rather uncommon. There is some inconvenience in having the burial or cremation the next morning, but it would be far outweighed by the advantage of having a true gathering of all those who knew and loved the deceased for a full celebration of the Eucharist. Parishes might want to discuss this pattern with funeral directors to work out practical details and to encourage them to suggest this option to families who consult with them.

Whenever the liturgy is held, there is a true need for the ministry of usher at funerals. Those gathering need to know which side is reserved for the family; ushers could encourage them to sit near the front on the other side and thus be able to support the family in song and prayer. When the funeral procession arrives, ushers can help to guide those who accompany the deceased to gather inside the church around the coffin for the welcoming rite. Ushers are also helpful to guide people at communion time and in the procession at the end. If a funeral is scheduled in the morning, perhaps one or two of the retired ushers could take on this ministry of hospitality.

Music for the Funeral Liturgy is always a challenge because those present will likely be from several parishes as well as from other faiths. An attractive booklet of hymns commonly used at funerals can be an invaluable participation aid, as can a program sheet that indicates each part of the liturgy, when to sit, stand, and kneel, and where to find musical selections.

There is a value to having members of the family or friends of the deceased involved as lectors, communion ministers, and gift bearers. That value is subordinate, however, to the importance of having these ministries carried out well. If a family member or friend is a trained lector or communion minister, they might well perform that ministry at the funeral. Those who are not trained for these ministries should not take them on just to have a way to be involved. Some of the mourners certainly could present the bread and wine, and family members might take a role is placing the pall on the casket. If some other Christian symbol is to be placed on the casket, that might also be done by a family member after the opening hymn while another speaks a brief explanation of the meaning of that symbol to the deceased (see #163 and #400).

Planners should make good pastoral use of the fifty-plus prayers for the dead in the rite and in #398. Many of these prayers are American creations to respond to the many varied ways that death comes.

The readings should be chosen in consultation with the mourners; they should focus attention clearly on the death and resurrection of the Lord and the promise of eternal life. The rite is very firm in insisting that the homily is not to be a eulogy. This rule is often violated, but the rite is quite clear: "there is never to be a eulogy" (#27). Preachers might meditate on that whole paragraph with its insights into the proper function of the homily during the funeral rites.

Communion often causes difficulties at funerals, since many may be present who are not Catholic. Pastoral sensitivity would suggest a brief announcement prior to communion, e.g., "We regret that the continued separation of the Christian churches does not permit us to share communion with those who are not Catholic, but we urge you to join us in prayer that one day soon we may be able to share from a common table."

The Funeral Liturgy concludes with the Final Commendation and Farewell. Though this rite may be moved to the place of committal, it seems best in most situations to celebrate it at church, so that those who do not go to the committal have an opportunity for saying farewell. As the body was sprinkled with water at the beginning, now it is surrounded with incense as a sign of respect and perhaps also a reminder of God's mercy that surrounds us. The song of farewell is the core of this rite. Parishes should choose a setting that is easily sung; one arranged in a responsory or echo form seems most workable.

The Rite of Committal

The *Order of Christian Funerals* reflects a strong preference that this rite be celebrated at the very site of committal, that is, at the grave or place of interment rather than at a cemetery chapel, if possible (#204). This means that the service will likely be outdoors, so the first task is to gather people closely enough to hear the presider and each other.

Once again, the rite calls for music as integral to the ritual: "a hymn or song that affirms hope in God's mercy and in the resurrection of the dead is desirable at the conclusion of the rite" (#214). The Lord's Prayer also might be sung.

If the Rite of Committal does not follow the Funeral Liturgy immediately (perhaps because the Liturgy was the previous evening or in another city), the Rite of Committal should be expanded with an opening song, readings, a sung psalm, and a homily (#211). If there has been no Funeral Liturgy, then the Rite of Committal with Final Commendation can be expanded in a similar way.

Conclusion

This chapter has provided only an overview of the rites available for celebrating a Christian funeral. There are numerous variations and adaptations in the *Order of Christian Funerals* that enable pastoral ministers to provide sensitive care in almost any situation. The number of options can be a bit overwhelming, which may be why some parishes fall into a set pattern that ignores the riches we have been given. What is needed is a commitment to become thoroughly familiar with the variations that are possible combined with a commitment to give our grieving brothers and sisters the best pastoral care we can offer. If we have the will, the *Order of Christian Funerals* gives us the way.

FUNERALS AND EVANGELIZATION

Eltin Griffin, O.Carm.

Preaching has to do with mystery. It has to do with the mystery of Christ as it applies to a particular celebration. The ultimate mystery for most people in our day is the mystery of death. In a world of such amazing and vast technological achievement, death is the great stumbling block. Thirty years ago, the *Pastoral Constitution on the Church in the Modern World* gave voice to this concern in an oft quoted paragraph (#18): "It is in regard to death that our condition is most shrouded in doubt. We are tormented not only by pain and the gradual breaking up of the body but also, and even more, by the dread of ceasing to be. But a deep instinct leads us rightly to shrink from and to reject the utter ruin and total loss of the personality. Because we bear within ourselves the seed of eternity which cannot be reduced to mere matter, we rebel against death. All aids, made available by technology, however useful they may be, cannot set our anguished minds at rest. They may prolong one's lifespan; but this does not satisfy the heart-felt longing, one that can never be stifled, for a life to come" (*Vatican*

Council II Documents, ed. Flannery, 1975. Adapted, with permission, to eliminate sexist language).

This is the background against which one preaches a homily at a funeral in our time. One views it, as it were, through the prism of Christ's own death and resurrection. One views it also through the prism of the Word of God chosen for the occasion. Funeral preaching provides a unique opportunity for evangelization. Persons who seldom visit a church, or who declare quite openly that they have no religious affiliation, will put in an appearance at the Funeral Mass or at the Vigil on the previous evening. Good preaching that brings the word to life and relates it to this particular occasion can have quite an impact. Communication, though, occurs at many other levels apart from the spoken word. The very way the presider introduces the celebration, his gestures, the vestments and how he wears them, their color, texture, and design, the way he invites the readers and others concerned, can make for communication at the deeper level of feeling. An evident healthy respect among the priest, the other ministers, and the gathered people will speak louder than the words. So can the atmosphere that emanates from a church or a parish where a developed sense of community and participation is evident. It is not a case of preaching only, but of preaching allied to witness. Pope John Paul II exhorts: "We need heralds of the gospel who are experts in humanity, who know the depths of the human heart, who can share the joys and the hopes, the agonies and distress of people today, who are at the same time contemplatives who have fallen in love with God. For this we need the saints of today."

Funeral Homilies

Homilies at funeral Masses can be problematic in some parishes where funerals tend to be frequent. It is difficult to be fresh on every occasion especially if, as sometimes happens, the funeral takes place at a late morning Mass that has its regular quota of attenders who may not be directly concerned with the obsequies. Here, too, the particular has to be merged with the general. The presider, in the Introduction to the *Order of Christian Funerals*, has been described as "a teacher of the faith and the minister of consolation." On him falls the burden of knitting the whole celebration together. One is celebrating the passing away, or more correctly, the passover, of a particular woman, man, or child.

The homily should never become a eulogy, but of course discreet allusion to the Christian witness of the deceased, or to the human qualities that endeared them to others, will not be out of place. Neither will a well-timed insertion of humor in regard to an older person, or a recall of personal characteristics, provided that the gist of the homily is centered on mystery. Not with the mystery of death itself, in the sense of why did one have to die. That can be sterile and can lead the hearers into an intellectual cul-de-sac. So can concern about life after death. Rather should the concern be with life through death, as happened with Christ, whose paschal mystery is the paradigm for a Christian's passing over to eternal life.

The Twist

What matters most in the special occasion homily is the particular twist that the preacher can give to it. A lot will depend upon the circumstances of the death and on the readings chosen for the occasion. Homilies given in tragic circumstances—suicide, accident, unexpected death, or the death of a child—can have enormous power if the Word suits the occasion. One picks up a lot of detail in a very short space of time as one visits the home, talks with the family, with neighbors, and with relatives.

The Word

The Lectionary offers a fairly good choice of readings. I have sometimes opted for the gospel of the previous Sunday.

A *Larger Package*

The homily, important though it may be, never stands on its own. It is part of a larger package. A friend of mine, a parish priest, traveled to some part of the United States to be with his brother in his illness and to celebrate the obsequies. He decided to check out the final details with the local church. He called the rectory only to be told that "Father says you'll find it all in the book." It is never all in the book. The book, admirable though it may be in many of its details, is more like the script of a play or the libretto of a musical to be rendered at the appropriate time and place. No two funeral services can ever be the same. One has always to adapt the rite to the occasion. One does not necessarily change anything, but the book as such offers a wide variety of options for prayers, prefaces, blessings, and readings. Like good stories, it all depends on the way you tell them. It all depends, too, on the way you read or proclaim the various items, on the accompanying gestures, and on the right pauses and emphases.

Music, for most people at a time of grief, can also make a big impact. Visiting musicians can wreck a service if they are not sensitive to the deeper spiritual meaning of the funeral rite and are able to choose music accordingly. One can only praise the efforts of parishes who try to provide an ad hoc weekday choir for funerals.

Compassion

Compassion is the heart of all Christian ministry, and more particularly, the heart of funeral ministry. With regard to the preaching, Henri J.M. Nouwen includes this little nugget somewhere: "What is addressed to the few gains the attention of the many."

NOVEMBER: UNITING MEMORY AND IMAGINATION IN HOPE

Dermot A. Lane

We are living at a time in which there is a serious eclipse of hope affecting the quality of political and religious life. At worst, there is an ever increasing amount of cynicism concerning the political process, and a growing apathy regarding religion. At best, there are traces of optimism in politics and religion. What is needed more than ever before is a strong, prophetic theology of hope that will disturb both church and society and transform their respective complacencies.

The month of November is a time when the Christian community remembers its dead. In particular, during November the church's liturgy celebrates the feast of All Saints, commemorates all the faithful departed, and previews in the Sunday readings the end of the world. The underlying assumption within the church's liturgy throughout November is the centrality of hope. Two of the most important elements within any theology of hope are memory and imagination. It is imagination that sparks off hope, and memory, which keeps hope alive. To be sure, there are other dimensions to hope, such as trust, love, story, and a creation-centered faith. In this short reflection we will confine ourselves to some preliminary remarks on the role of memory and the place of imagination in the birth of hope, in view of their liturgical importance for the month of November.

The Power of Memory

Contemporary philosophy and theology have rehabilitated the importance of memory to a remarkable degree. Memory is an important ingredient in the construction of human identity and the shaping of human consciousness. A balanced understanding of who we are arises out of our capacity to be connected through memory with the past. Memory enables the past to influence the present. To remember is to make alive what has been cut off from us through death.

The kind of memory we are talking about here is not that which simply recalls the good old days, nor is it merely the memory that indulges sentimentally in some past golden age. Instead it is the memory that is true to the past in a manner that has power to disrupt and interrupt the coziness of the present. It is the memory that has the capacity to interrupt the tyranny of the present. Above all, the memory in question is one that enables us to realize that the way we are is not the way we have to be; it is a memory that has the ability to activate a praxis that breaks through the prevailing historical consciousness as if it were an irreformable given.

To remember the dead as we do in November is to make alive again those who have been cut off from us. This process of remembering is about putting back together what has been dismembered from us. By remembering the dead we recover something of the fundamental unity and solidarity of the whole human family. This sense of unity between the living and the dead—which is symbolized through the Christian doctrine of the Communion of Saints and perhaps more fully by the commemoration of all the dead—is an important step in the genesis of hope. I cannot hope alone—but I can begin to hope in solidarity with the dead and the living.

It is instructive to note in passing how the dead have been remembered in the past through monuments like Newgrange in Ireland and the pyramids in Egypt—powerful symbols of ancestral unity.

To disconnect ourselves from the past is to cut ourselves off from one of the important sources of human identity. We are what we are in virtue of our dead. Those who sever their solidarity with the dead all too quickly end up severing their solidarity with the living. This, in turn, leads to hopeless forms of individualism symbolized in the self-sufficiency of modern self. In contrast, Gabriel Marcel points out:"Hope is only possible on the level of us, or we might say *agape* ... it does not exist on the level of the solitary ego" (G. Marcel, *Homo Viator: An Introduction to a Metaphysic of Hope* London: V. Gollancz, 1951]10). A close correlation seems to exist between the rise of individualism and the eclipse of hope today.

Memory in the Judeo-Christian Tradition

It is no mere coincidence that memory plays a crucial role in the life of Judaism and Christianity. Judaism is about remembering the passover experience and God's covenant with the people of Israel. Likewise in Christianity it is the memory of the crucified and risen Christ, celebrated in the Eucharist, that sustains the Christian community in hope. The memory of Jesus, his preaching about the reign of God, his open table-fellowship, his unconditional offer of forgiveness, and especially his saving death and resurrection, activate hope in the present and the future. This memory of Jesus is often described as a liberating, dangerous, and disturbing memory.

The most appropriate place, therefore, for the Christian to remember the dead is in the celebration of the Eucharist. In the Eucharist we remember the dead no longer as dead but as alive in Christ, no longer as past but as present to us in the Christian assembly. In the Eucharist, through the memory of the passion, death, and resurrection of Christ, our unity with the past is recovered, hope in the present is renewed, and the future is anticipated. When we celebrate the Eucharist, the pastness of the dead and the deadness of the past are transformed into a new dynamic reality in the present that shapes our understanding of the future. It is this extraordinary power of memory, particularly effective in the Eucharist, that generates hope. If it is true to say that memory is an important ingredient in the genesis of hope, then it is equally true to assert that it is imagination that sustains hope in existence.

The Role of Imagination

When imagination becomes dulled or deadened, or when the imagination finds itself caught in between paradigm shifts, which represents our present experience, then one of the first casualties is hope. A close connection exists between imagination and hope.

In talking about imagination, we need to get away from the popular misunderstanding that imagination is about the fanciful projection of an unreal world. To the contrary, imagination is about the human capacity to construct a coherent world of meaning out of the connections that exist between a variety of different images. Imagination is about knowing and understanding the world around us. In particular, imagination is about the capacity to construct new and alternative possibilities out of our experience of the world in which we live. It is this innate and irrepressible capacity to image life differently and alternatively that keeps hope in existence. It is important, therefore, to distinguish between the fanciful imagination and the realistic imagination.

The imagination that sustains hope in existence is not the private imagination of the isolated individual but the imagination that is in touch with other configurations of the world in which we live. When the private imagination of the individual predominates, there is always the danger of despair, that is, a sense of total aloneness that can overwhelm. As William Lynch sums up: "What happens in despair is that the private imagination, of which we are so enamored, reaches the point of the end of inward resource and must put on the imagination of another if it is to find a way out" (William F. Lynch, *Images of Hope: Imagination as Healer of the Hopeless* [Notre Dame, IN: University of Notre Dame Press, 1965] 23). Hope, which is really a response to the inner temptation of despair, arises when my little imagination is enlarged by the imagination of others. Thus the exchange of images, stories of different accounts of the world, is the catalyst activating the dynamism of hope. It is only in and through the collaboration, or mutuality, of imaginations, that hope can emerge and transform the temptation to despair. It is this alternative imaging of the world by the other that enables hope to transcend the suffocating particularity of one's own private imagination. The imagination that heals the hopeless is the imagination expanded by interacting with the imaginations of others.

At present the religious imagination is going through a particularly parched period in the history of its existence, and this may be due to its isolation from the artistic, literary, and scientific imaginations. There is something of an irony in the fact that, at a time when the religious imagination is in decline, the scientific imagination is on the increase. The time has come when a new dialogue between the religious and scientific imaginations should take place if the much needed transformation of the present eclipse of hope is to take place.

A Peep at the Scientific Imagination

Some will balk at this new dialogue because the scientific imagination of the modern era did not serve the religious imagination well. In fact, many would argue that the modern scientific imagination squeezed God out of the world through the mechanization of nature and the secularizing of the self and society. Is it possible that some aspects of the post-modern scientific imagination might act as a midwife to a revitalization of the religious imagination? Let me suggest in mere outline two examples from the scientific imagination in which this might begin to happen.

The new cosmic story, coming from astrophysics and contemporary cosmologies, is helping humanity to rediscover the fundamental unity of everything in the world, with particular reference to the exquisite unity that obtains between the cosmos, the earth, and the self. This new cosmic story tells us that the human self is the earth and the cosmos in a state of self-conscious freedom. The images of living in "a finely tuned universe," of being part of "a cosmic dance," of participating in "a symphony of life," might well help the religious imagination to discover the meaning of social solidarity, ecological responsibility, and interpersonal communion. Religion needs to rediscover these basic ideas if it is to redesign an inclusive theology of hope pertinent to the present and capable at the same time of imaging the future.

A second example might be taken from what the scientific imagination has to say about human origins. Contemporary scientists, in the light of the new story about the evolution of the cosmos, talk about human beings as children of cosmic dust: "We are all made of the ashes of dead stars" (J. Polkinghorne, *One World: The Interaction of Science and Theology* [London: SPCK, 1986] 56). If the scientific imagination is able to move from cosmic dust to human beings in this way, surely the Christian religious imagination should be able to talk credibly about the transformation of human dust into a new creation in Christ.

Of course there is a radical difference between the imagination of science and the imagination of religion. They deal with different subject matter, different sources of meaning, and different methodologies. Equally important, it must be emphasized, is that religion must resist the temptation of tying its particular insights to any one specific scientific hypothesis. There can be no doubt that current scientific theories will change in the future and, to this extent, theology cannot be tied to any one particular scientific theory. However, these differences between the scientific and religious imagination—and they are significant—will only emerge when the conversation begins. In the meantime, the isolation of the religious imagination needs to be transformed by interaction with the scientific imagination.

One place where this dialogue might take place is in the search for hope in our world today. A productive context in which this search for hope should be made explicit is the month of November in which we honor and remember our dead. By remembering the dead, with hope for them and ourselves, we need the help of the imagination to go beyond the cynicism and apathy that are characteristic of so much politics and religion today.

Part Two

SAMPLE HOMILIES

Death of an Older Person

SELF-SURRENDER

Eltin Griffin, O. Carm.

READING: LK 22:44–49

There is an old Irish story about a tailor in County Clare. He had a large family and had to work very hard to support them. He didn't have much time for prayer but every time he pierced a piece of cloth and drew the needle he whispered "O Jesus, pierce with your mercy the hearts of all poor sinners who are going to die in the world today." Tailoring has advanced a great deal since then. Technology has caught up with it. But it is still a beautiful trade, working on fabric. It requires enormous concentration. It is a very creative work. The master tailor is more than a tradesman. He is a craftsman and an artist. The end product is always distinctive and a work of art. It is not only a creative art; it is also recreating. Allied to a happy home life, it can lead to great contentment, composure of spirit, and a contemplative outlook on life. It can lead to a very high quality of life and living. However, the greater the quality of life, the harder it is to part with it. We see it in the case of Jesus himself, the struggle that engaged him in Gethsemane when everything seemed a failure in the face of death. The struggle on the cross when he cried out in utter desolation "My God, My God, why have you forsaken me?" There is a hymn used in the Mass of Easter Sunday, a sequence that is sung before the gospel, the *Victimae Paschali*, which puts this struggle in a nutshell:

> Death and life contended
> combat strangely ended.

Death, let's face it, is disintegration. There is the struggle to part with what is the most precious thing of all, and that is life itself. And yet, it is the most total act of self-surrender, of self-giving. It brings together into one all the acts of self-giving, of self-surrender, of commitment to the Lord and to others that we have made in this life. Dying, as one French spiritual writer puts it, is one's own little Mass. The church puts on our lips at night prayer, "Father into your hands I commend my spirit."

Joe made his final act of self-surrender at 2:05 on Friday last, surrounded by a loving family who had kept vigil with him for several days. But he didn't give up too easily. He had that strength of steel that was part of his stock and trade. He wanted nothing else at his funeral but lots of singing. Such a humble self-effacing man, he would not be a bit too pleased at my eulogizing his virtues here this morning. He said to his son before being admitted to the Meath Hospital, "Face your father's death, son. You will find it the most purifying experience of your life." What a man of faith!

I have attended many a dying person in my time, but Joe was the first ever to ask me to read a poem for him and he was quite low on that particular day. His favorite poet was Yeats, and one poem he obviously loved was the "Fiddler of Dooney." "You'll find it," he said to me, "on page 34."

When we come at the end of time,
To Peter sitting in state,
He will smile on the three old spirits,
But call me first through the gate.,

For the good are always the merry
Save by an evil chance,
And the merry love the fiddle
And the merry love to dance:

And when the folk there spy me,
They will all come up to me,
With "Here is the Fiddler of Dooney!"
And dance like a wave of the sea.

Death of an Older Person

HARVEST TIME

Aidan Ryan

READINGS: GAL 5:22–25; LK 8:4–15

In this part of the country, a word that's rarely used is the word "autumn." Instead, people refer to the August-October period as "harvest." There is an air of fullness and completion about this time of year, an atmosphere that the poet Keats described with the phrase "mists and mellow fruitfulness."

Today we celebrate the Funeral Mass of TJ in this atmosphere of mellowness, fruitfulness, fullness, and completion. We come to give God thanks for a long life, a life filled with the fruits of the Holy Spirit—love, joy, peace, patience, kindness, faithfulness, and gentleness—the harvest of a life well lived.

Death is sometimes described in literature, or depicted in art, as the "Grim Reaper," a kind of skeletal ghost that comes with a sharp scythe to mow us down. But that is not how Christian faith sees death. The Christian vision is much better expressed, I think, in the well-known Irish poem, *Ag Críost an Síol:*

51

Christ's is the seed and Christ's the harvest.
May we be gathered into God's barn.

Christ sowed the seed of eternal life many years ago in TJ when
he was brought as an infant to (this) church for his baptism, or to
use the more popular local word, his christening, his first and
greatest bonding into union with Christ. In all the years that have
passed since then, Christ tended that seed as it grew. He nourished
the tender seeds of his young Christian life in his first confession
and communion and confirmation. Christ saw that seed come to
full bloom in TJ's adult life, in his marriage and his rearing of his
family. Christ saw the growth of that seed into a ripe old age. And
now, in the fullness of his time, Christ has gathered to himself the
rich abundant harvest of a long and fruitful life.

No matter how long a life is, there is still a great sadness in
death, especially for those who have to bid even a temporary
farewell to a dearly loved father and grandfather, a good neighbor,
a cherished friend. But our faith makes us hopeful today as we
look forward to the time when God's harvesting will be complete,
and we will all be gathered together with him and with those we
have loved, to be happy forever in the kingdom of God's eternal
love.

Death of an Older Person

"IT IS A HOLY AND A WHOLESOME THOUGHT TO PRAY FOR THE DEAD"

Brendan McConvery, C.Ss.R.

READINGS: 2 MACC 12:43–45; PS 103;
ROM 6:3–9; MT 25:31-46

Kathleen has gone to join the "holy souls" whom she always considered as close friends. No rosary was ever said without a prayer for the dead. At every Mass, she had a list of departed friends and neighbors that lengthened with every year that passed. It was not simply a list. Each had a name and a face, and a memory of some act of kindness to be repaid with a prayer. The anniversaries of the family dead were never forgotten. November was her special time. It began at Halloween, as she so often told us of how, when she was young, her granny would bring her to visit the church in the evening of All Saints. Six times the "Our Father," "Hail Mary," and "Glory Be." Many visits were packed into that half-hour. Then back home in the twilight, the young girl and the old woman, happy in the confidence that their prayers had brought some recently deceased neighbor, or a poor forgotten one with no-one to pray for them, past the ever-vigilant Peter straight to the waiting embrace of Mary and her son.

Kathleen was a quiet and a gentle woman. The only things she probably had in common with the warrior Judas, who was praised in the first reading, is that, like him, in all this, she took full account of the resurrection. She was brought up with unwavering certainty that it was a holy and a wholesome thought to pray for the dead that they may be released from their sins. It was a belief she never lost, and with it went a hope that she would be remembered in the prayers of those she left behind. There was another woman once who had the same sort of faith as Kathleen. The story of her death, written by her son, is one of the most moving pages of Christian writing. He was the great Augustine, she was St. Monica. Monica died far from home, but she did not want a lavish funeral. As she told Augustine, who had so often scalded her heart, "Lay this body wherever it may be. Let no care of it disturb you. This alone do I ask of you, that you remember me at the altar of God." For Kathleen, the boundary walls between heaven and earth were never very thick, but they were at their thinnest at the time of the celebration of the Eucharist. It was truly a moment of living communion of the saints. We are honoring the request in a very special way now, but I think she would want us to remember her always at the altar of God.

Prayer for the dead is deeply ingrained in our Catholic tradition, and expresses in a simple way some of the deepest truths of our faith. It expresses first of all our utter certainty that the faithful departed are in God's sure keeping and that nothing can take them from his hand. It also expresses our confidence in a merciful God who respects our efforts, and does not demand any more of us than we are able to give.

In the gospel, we listened to Matthew's account of the final judgment. St. John of the Cross caught the essence of that account when he remarked that "in the evening of life, we will be judged on love." The test of love is to have fed the hungry, clothed the naked, to have made a place in our hearts for the forgotten and the rejected. Our education in love began at baptism, when, as St. Paul puts it, we were plunged into the mystery of the death and resurrection of Christ. It is a lesson so vital that we spend the rest of our lives learning its truth. Some people are wonderfully quick at picking it up. Most of us, though, have to admit that we are slow learners. We may not be conscious of great sin, but often, there is a meanness, a stinginess, and a fear of the cost of being generous in the love we show to others. Our traditional belief in purgatory sometimes compared it to the familiar experience of a child who has failed in her schoolwork and has to stay behind to do extra lessons. The time of detention may not last very long, but for the child who wants to play in the sunlight with her friends, every moment can seem like hours. We really do not know how long the lesson of purgatory lasts. It could be simply the moment when, as we enter the presence of the Lord in death, we become aware of just how often and how meanly we have failed, but that all that failure of ours is transformed by the resurrection of Jesus.

GOING HOME

Ambrose Tinsley, O.S.B.

READING: JN 14:1–6

"Do not let your hearts be troubled." These are good words for such a moment as this. When someone dies, especially a person who has been a part of our own lives for many, many years, there is not just a sense of emptiness but also the disturbing presence of unanswerable questions, even if we do not put them into words. Our mood is constantly sad, as is the color of the clothes we tend to wear. Indeed, if we who come around the altar to concelebrate this Mass have chosen purple vestments, rather than the white ones which are sometimes used, it is because they symbolize the grieving, with so many questions unresolved, which are inevitable stages of our journey here on earth. And so, we sympathize in a very special way with Pauline and her family for whom May has, for so long, meant so much.

They called her Auntie May. Indeed, the first time I met her she was getting off a bus to visit Pauline and her family as she so often did. Their house for May in those days was a second home and, later, when her own strength was failing, she accepted their invitation to remain with them. I often chatted with her there. I consequently know that sometimes she could feel that she was just a nuisance and a burden, but I also know that never did she cease to be a loved and valued person in their home.

But now she has gone to another home. Her going, when it actually happened, was a quiet, almost unexpected one. The Hindu people, I am told, refer to death as but the quenching of a lamp because the dawn has come. May's death was just like that. It was the silent stopping of a candle flame, and she now knows, in a way that we do not, why she does not require it any more. For her the dawn of that new day, the day that shall not ever end, has come. The light that she possesses now is that of Christ himself, the Risen One, and so the warmth and happiness of his eternal home is hers.

But let us come back for a moment to the gospel that we have just heard. It tells us that before his own departure Christ had said to his disciples: "I am going to prepare a place for you."' He wanted them to know that, after he had left them, he would do all that he could to make it possible for them to follow and to be with him again. Can we now not say the same of May? Has she not gone to share in her own way in that same work of Christ? Is she not now preparing an important place for those who have already done so much for her? I'm sure she is and I am sure that those who loved her in this present life will find that in the life to come one of their very special joys will be enjoying it with her.

Of course we have no adequate idea of what that life, which is ahead of us, is going to be like. The Scriptures sometimes speak about it as a meal or banquet to which everyone is called, and sometimes as a paradise in which there will be no more tears or pain of any kind. They also say, and this may be encouraging considering our black or purple clothes, that in our life we will be robed in white. That surely is an image filled with hope, although we still have to admit that the reality will far outstrip what those "white robes" imply.

However, as we keep on yearning for what is to come, those who knew Auntie May throughout her earthly life have many reasons to be certain that their future is in good and well-experienced hands.

Death of an Older Person

THE GRAIN FALLS

Benedict Hegarty, O.P.

READINGS: 2 TIM 4:6–8; JN 12:20–26

There can be lives full of possibility that are cut off in their youth. We are left wondering what way they would go; how things would have turned out for them; and we are saddened by all that could have happened and now is lost forever. In the case of our friend (name), it is all different. For her, her days among us were lengths of years and joy. Every indicator says she lived a long, happy, and fulfilled life.

She died in the autumn of her life. Each season of the year has its own beauty. Spring has its, with its superabundance of life and growth. Well wrapped up in winter, we can appreciate the trees and bushes glittering with frost; the mantle of snow covering ugliness; the warmth, welcome, comfort of homes. Summer is a tranquil season. It is a time for holidays, slowing down of the tempo of days, long evenings, bright mornings. Autumn has its special beauty. A poet once described it in the following words:

Season of mists and mellow fruitfulness,
Close bosom-friend of the maturing sun.

It is a time of harvest and fruitfulness. The trees look spectacular in their autumn garb.

There is an autumn in life too. The good fight has been fought. Energies are declining but with that come the shedding of responsibilities and much contentment. Many people shy off from the very thought of it, but the poet had another angle. He could see the riches, the achievement, the color, the contentment of autumn. That too is the experience of many people as they grow older: they are calm, peaceful, fulfilled, happy, rich in relationships and maturity.

There was something of the autumn with all its special goodness about the last years of (name). There was a basic contentment and peace. There was a sense of duty done, life lived, love given and received.

Autumn signals the end of an age of life. In the flaming forests, life is declining and winter is about to set in. Decline is not the whole story, however. Dead leaves are falling to the ground but they are not alone. The seeds of new life are also falling. Jesus thought of this when he spoke of the grain of wheat. It falls into the ground; it seems to die but in the act of dying and being received into the earth it gives birth to the green sprout, beautiful and bountiful. In the winds and storms of autumn the seeds are shaken from the branches. Sometimes they are caught by a gentle breeze; other times, it is a violent storm that snatches them, whirls them through the air. In the end, they fall to the welcoming earth, which is ready to receive them and is life-giving. Dying is part of living and a step along the road of ongoing life.

When autumn comes in life, it is also difficult to let go. Letting go can be painful and long, or short and quick. But having let go, (name's) spirit did not flutter off into darkness. Every Sunday we profess our faith in the resurrection of Jesus of Nazareth. In doing so we also proclaim our faith in a new life for every man, woman, and child from the beginning to the end of human history. That is our routine faith. The statement of belief is said so often. "We look for the resurrection of the dead." It is our everyday faith and then there comes the day when these words take on a deep personal message for us. Such a moment is now when we are laying to rest one whom we knew in our different ways—a parent, spouse, friend, neighbor. Then the words "we look for the resurrection of the dead" take on a new meaning.

There are many choices to make in life as there are many great events in life. Life ends with the greatest event of all. When we have done everything that God has mapped out for us in the space of life he has given us; when the autumn and harvest of achievement has arrived, then it is time to hand ourselves back to him in a last homecoming.

So it was with (name). In the autumn of her life, she released her spirit to God, was received by his welcoming love, and was made ready for a new spring in God's life-filled presence forever.

Death of an Older Person

BLESSING AND FAITHFULNESS

Brian McKay, O. Carm.

READINGS: IS 25:6–9; PS 23; REV 21:1–7; JN 14:1–6

We gather in this holy place today to bid farewell to N., to pray for the repose of his soul, and to pray for the consolation of those who mourn N.'s passing from this world. Death is always a shock. No matter how inevitable the end may be, we always experience an acute pain when one whom we have loved dearly passes from our midst. At a sad time like this, what can we hold onto that will help to ease the pain?

First, we recall that N. enjoyed a long life and received many blessings and graces from God down through the years. *(Here, mention some points of relevance from the person's life.)* For these blessings, we give thanks and praise to God.

Second, we remember N.'s faithfulness. The great virtue in the Old Testament was the virtue of faithfulness, that is, sticking to one's convictions through thick and thin, and this can easily be said of N. His devotion to his family, to his religion, which he cherished so much, to his friends, was an example from which we can all learn. Perhaps today he wants us to stop and consider how great our faithfulness to our faith is, how great is our commitment to Our Lord Jesus Christ.

Third, we can be consoled today by our memories of N. Memory is a truly wonderful thing, for at will we can recall incidents and events that make us realize just how special and unique a person N. was. *(Again here it is good to share some appropriate facet of the person's life.)* What is even more wonderful again is the fact that how we remember N. is the way he is in the eternal present of God's presence. It is true to say that for N. time as we know it has stopped, for his existence is on a new shore in closer communion with God.

Finally, there is much consolation to be had from the beauty of the liturgy itself. In times past, death was something to be greatly feared because of the harshness of a judgmental God. Our liturgy today presents us with the love, mercy, and compassion of a kind and caring God. The prophet Isaiah reminds us that the time will come when every tear will be wiped away and when God will gather all his loved ones together to celebrate a great feast. Psalm 23 powerfully acknowledges that God is a loving shepherd who will welcome N. home and who will watch over him for all eternity. In the Book of Revelation, we read that there will be no more death and no more mourning or sadness, and, as we have already noted, John's gospel speaks of there being room for all who believe that Jesus Christ is the Way, the Truth, and the Life.

Today then, we bid farewell to N. Despite our sense of loss, we face the future with courage and hope, knowing that that is what N. would want us to do. We comfort one another in the sure confidence that for N. life has changed, not ended, as the Preface of the Mass expresses it. We also derive comfort from the conviction that N. is at peace with God.

Death of a Young Person

CANDYFLOSS

Richard Sheehy

READING: 2 TIM 4:6–8

"I have fought the good fight to the end, I have run the race to the finish, I have kept the faith." These words of St. Paul beautifully sum up Bridget's life, and particularly her last year. Since February, Bridget has lived with and waged a courageous battle against cancer. It's a battle that in the end she lost, but she put up a great fight.

Over these past fourteen months, Bridget had to overcome many hurdles: there was the shock of the initial diagnosis, the prospect of chemotherapy, the side effects of the treatment, the return of the cancer just when she thought she was getting better, and eventually her being confined to bed.

At each of these setbacks, she had moments of doubt, of anger, fear, and even despair. Bridget didn't hide her feelings at such moments, but they were always of short duration. What impressed me about her was the way she bounced back so quickly, set herself new goals, and got on with the struggle. She could accept the limitations her illness imposed on her and still manage to enjoy life. She never lost her sense of humor, or her interest in what was going on around her, and she hated to feel that she was being left out of anything. Nothing was allowed to escape her attention. I remember a couple of months ago she wrote a list of questions for the doctor in the hospital. I'm sure he was taken aback to find himself on the receiving end of a rigorous cross-examination.

Bridget's greatest strength in her illness was the love and support of her family. She confided to me on more than one occasion how much this meant to her. Everyone rallied round and gave her constant encouragement. Bridget's room became the focal point in the house. It's a tribute, too, to the kind of person that she was that Bridget had such loyal and devoted friends.

She was conscious of the demands her illness made on her family. At times she could be impatient or irritable, but I know she always regretted it immediately. Home meant everything to her, and she could have wished for nothing more than to spend her final days there surrounded by the people she loved.

Bridget would not want me to eulogize her. I can almost hear her telling me to cut the ... candyfloss! (Only the word she would use would be even more colorful!) But I know she would want me to assure her mother and father, her family and friends, that she is with God and that she is happy.

It's hard to understand why she had to die so young. It is perhaps a consolation to know that Our Lord himself has shared Bridget's experience. For Bridget, as for Jesus himself, the race ended prematurely. As with the life of Our Lord there will always be the feeling that there was so much more Bridget could have done, so much more that life had to offer her, so much more she would have liked to do, if only circumstances had been kinder. It was not to be.

But if we are sad today, there is also much to be thankful for. We are grateful for the life she did have, grateful for all the joy she brought into our lives. For you, her family, there's the comfort of knowing that you were able to show Bridget over the past year just how much you all loved and appreciated her. You knew that time was precious. All that you could have done for her, you did. There are no regrets.

A few weeks ago we celebrated our belief that Christ is risen from the dead and has conquered death. Today we believe that Bridget is sharing in that resurrection:

> I am the resurrection and the life.
> He who believes in me,
> even though he dies,
> will live forever;
> and whoever lives and believes in me
> will never die.

This was Bridget's faith, a faith that was personal but deep. This is the faith that we as a community celebrate in our Mass this morning. It is the faith that comforts us in our sorrow.

Bridget, you fought the good fight to the end. You ran the race to the finish. You kept the faith. May you now enter into the joy of eternal life.

Amen.

Death of a Young Person

"HE SHALL NOT GROW OLD"

Brendan McConvery, C.Ss.R.

READINGS: WIS 4:7–15; PS 23; 1 JN 3:14–16; JN 11:32–45

Fewer burdens are heavier than the coffin of your son, your younger brother, or your best friend on your shoulder. Our hearts go out today to Liam's family, and to the friends who shared the adventure of his young manhood. In our grief, we have listened as the gospel unfolded the story of another young man's death. John tells us so little about Lazarus and his two sisters that he seems to invite us to read between the lines. In Jesus' time, when marriage at a young age was the norm, a family of two sisters and a brother, with no sign of parents, husbands, or wives in the background might lead us to suspect that the main actors in the story were three young unmarried people, doing their best to get on with the business of life. Their chain of dreams and hopes depended on the support of one another. That chain is now cruelly broken by death. They had wanted so desperately for him to get well. Over the weeks of Liam's illness, his family prayed the words of the message the sisters sent to Jesus, "Lord, the one you love, the one we love, is sick." We can understand if their grief finds an echo in Mary's reproach to Jesus, "Lord, if you had been here, my brother would not have died."

When someone as young as Liam is taken from us, we ask the question "why did it have to be he?" The answer to a question like this will not come simply by dint of thinking. It has to be distilled from life's experience, from grief and, above all, from time and memory.

We grieve today that a life full of promise seems to have been cut short. Yet, as the first reading reminds us, life's flourishing cannot be reckoned by the passing of years alone. A poet, who was overwhelmed by the thought of so many young lives lost on the battlefields of World War I, tried to come to terms with so much death when peace finally came:

They shall not grow old, as we who are left grow old.
Age shall not weary them, nor the years condemn.
At the rising of the sun and in the morning,
We shall remember them.
(Lawrence Binyon: *For the Fallen*)

For almost eighty years now, those words have brought consolation to the families of the fallen. Jesus believed that through the illness and death of Lazarus the glory of God would be revealed. As people who believe in the resurrection, we dare to profess our faith that the death of this young man will show us, in time, something of God's glory. In Liam's short life and tragic death, the Lord may also be gracing us with a glimpse of what eternal life means.

The English writer Graham Greene lived to be over eighty. In the last interview he gave, to a journalist who visited him some months before his death, he was asked whether his Catholic faith in eternal life made the prospect of death any more welcome. Greene replied that he found the prospect of a life that simply went on forever boring. Like most of us, Greene was baffled by the phrase "eternal life." In trying to understand it, he put the stress on the first word. But "eternity" is a word too big for our minds to grasp. The only way we can imagine it is by trying to imagine time stretching out forever. The liveliest party, the most exhilarating hiking expedition or rock concert that goes on too long, ends up by becoming boring. It might be easier to pierce the mystery of eternal life by beginning with the word "life." When we think of Liam at his best, we think of a young man brimming over with irrepressible energy, with promise, with laughter. He was someone who never lost the capacity to surprise us. He was never predictable. He will be forever fixed in our memory and in our hearts as someone who was not crushed by the burdens of life, even by his last illness. He was not made cynical by dreams that never fulfilled their promise, or made cautious by bitter experience. That may be his parting gift to us, a reminder that life is exuberant and ever youthful. If it is eternal, then it will be ever new, ever full of surprises, bursting with a promise that there is more to come.

Soon we shall carry the body of Liam, washed with holy water and perfumed with incense, to its final resting place. There we will confide him to the care of the Lord who wept by the tomb of Lazarus his friend. Let us do it in the hope of the final words, "Unbind him, and let him go free."

Death of a Young Person

WHOLENESS
AND HOLINESS

Brian McKay, O. Carm.

READINGS: WIS 4:7-15; PS 23; THESS 4:13-18; MT 11:25-30

The news of N.'s death was a message that shocked and saddened all who knew N. We could scarcely believe it then—we can scarcely believe it now. We have lost a valued and loved member of our community and, really, we are trying to make sense of an aspect of human life that is so difficult to understand. We do not know why God has taken N. at this young age and, probably, we will never comprehend it this side of the grave. Today, we need to ask ourselves if there is anything that we can hold onto to help us through this time of grief, something to help us cope with the feeling of darkness, the feeling of a bright light having been extinguished.

There is the memory of N. himself, his personality, his talents, his achievements, the gift that he was to his family, to his friends, to his school (university, job) and to his local community. *(Here it is good to make direct reference to the person's life.)* For N. was a gift who helped spread God's love everywhere he went during his short life, and for the gift of this young person, we give thanks and praise to God. We are all the better for ever having known him.

Our gospel today extends an invitation to each one of us to "come to me, all you who labor and are overburdened and I will give you rest." We believe that N. is being taken care of. We who are left behind must take care of each other and, in so doing, God's healing power will be at work among us to give us strength, consolation, and courage for the future. Remembering N., his good points, his weaknesses, his talents, his personality, will be very important for everyone over the next few weeks and months. The memory of a person no longer with us can be a very powerful aid to our coping with a distressing and inexplicable situation. The memory of a person can help us to get on with our own lives as, indeed, we must.

Those of us left behind may also need to learn something from N.'s life and death. N.'s passing from us may show us that life is a gift, something very precious, something that each of us should value and cherish. Sometimes, we need to be reminded that life is good and worth putting effort into. Perhaps that is a message that N. would like us to hear today.

I wonder what message N. would like to impart to us today as he keeps an eye on our doings. I think he would want us all to be strong, determined, unafraid of the future, ready to meet every challenge—to believe in ourselves and to try and keep believing in God, even if that seems to be difficult at this time.

Finally, we wish again to extend our deepest sympathy to all N.'s family and friends. We know that these days are most traumatic. By our presence we want to say to you that we are grieving with you and will do all we can to support you over the next few days, weeks, months. The Lord Jesus says, "I am the resurrection and the life. If anyone believes in me, even though he dies, yet will he live." N. is with God; N. is at peace.

Death of a Young Person

"THEY HAVE TAKEN (MY LORD) AWAY"

Betty Maher

READING: JN 19:25–27

As we face the sorrow and loneliness of today, and of the days and weeks and months ahead, perhaps—not now, but a little later—we may find some comfort in remembering that on the day of Jesus' death, Mary, too, knew the kind of pain that (we) are experiencing here today. There were more than three crucifixions on that day, because no mother could stand below the cross of her child and not feel that she herself was being crucified.

Jesus, like all of us when we are in physical pain, must have felt his own suffering. And therefore, as I see it, it was an extraordinary example of human love and pity—pity in the best sense of the word—that moved Jesus to become aware of the pain of his mother who stood alongside him, and to momentarily forget his own pain, in order to look for some way in which he could ease that pain for her.

For us here today, there is just such pain, and there are also questions. (Even though we may have known that N.'s death was expected, we are still left with questions.)

But when someone dies who is young—a baby, or someone who is living a full and busy life, with youth and beauty on their side, and is suddenly and inexplicably cut down—then the questions seem to multiply.

Jesus, too, died in the prime of life; and Mary was his mother. How could she hope to understand what was happening? Is there any way to deal with this sort of shock, and the pain attached? I think that to find a fitting answer one would have to be God.

At the very time when he was suffering most, Jesus, in the fullness and vulnerability of his humanity, must have felt as inadequate as many of us no doubt do today. He was looking at his grieving mother and was unable to take her pain away. So too, we are helpless in the face of death, to "make it all right."

And so Jesus did the best he could manage; he looked for a way in which his mother's future life might in some way be eased. (One interpretation I have read of this story suggests that just as Mary influenced the early years of Jesus and gave him direction, so now he gave her direction for her future life—life without him— just when it must have seemed to her that, as his life's blood drained away, so did hers also.)

And for this he needed the cooperation of his friend. And he got it. John's response to Jesus when he was asked to look after Mary, must have been a real chink of light for Jesus himself at that moment, as he neared his last breath.

Although his own pain was drawing to an end, Jesus knew that Mary would have to endure. In the natural order of things she would not have seen his death. He was facing the loneliness of death by himself, and he knew that she would have to do the same, as all of us must. This, I believe, adds to the pain of everyone when someone they love dies. It is the loneliness of the human condition.

But this is also, I like to think, the very reason why we can hope; we can surely hope that some day such loneliness will finally be over, and we will experience reunion in love.

And so, today, just as Mary went as far as she could with her dying son, so we too can only try to walk with one another, and especially with those whose loss is greatest. We will feel inadequate, that's for sure, but by sharing in—so far as we can— the pain of those who most deeply mourn, we can try our best to "be Christ" to one another. Our inadequacy, our sheer human clumsiness, is part of being human, I am sure—but it is well to remember too that this very lack is part of the reason why we can continue to hope; to hope that a time will come, for all of us, when such inadequacies will be no more.

Mary's faith and love saw her through the crucifixion of her only child. As we move along this lonely road today, let us pray for one another, that we will find in the love of those nearest to us the love and support that Jesus asked of John toward his mother, and which he also asked of Mary toward the Beloved Disciple.

Death of a Young Person

HAVE NO FEAR

John Wall

READINGS: WIS 4:7–15; PS 48 1–13; 2 COR 5:1; 6–10; MT 25:31–40

When Mother Teresa of Calcutta used to quote this gospel, as she did frequently, it seemed to make a lot of sense to a lot of people —even to those who were not, as we might put it, "into"religion. It simply says that at the end of the day we're judged on love, on how we treated each other. For that reason Brian need have no fear as he goes before his God. His life was built on love. And he, in turn, was—and is—greatly loved himself.

This Mass is a sad occasion for all of us. It is also a "eucharist," a celebration of thanksgiving for Brian's life. And there is much to be grateful for. Last evening I talked to Brian's mother and father and family, and together we prepared this liturgy. As they spoke, I was struck by the amount of echoes of today's gospel, of goodness to other people, that were evident in his life. I'm sure each one of you here will have had your own memories of Brian as you have sat and swapped your own stories, as people do at times like this.

He packed so much into his short life. As our first reading put it: "Being perfected in a short time, he fulfilled long years, for his soul was pleasing to the Lord."

As with most young people, music was very important in his life. Brian would go along with the response to our psalm today: "I will solve my problem with the harp," or in his case, with his guitar. I think we can begin to take in the *big* fact of death slowly as an inevitable natural fact of life. But isn't it true to say that it's those *small* things, like seeing his guitar, that make our tears flow? And tears are healthy and natural. Jesus himself wept at the death of his good friend Lazarus.

Bereavement is the price of love. When a person is greatly loved then that person will be greatly missed. So at times like this we have a great need of love and kindness and concern and a rallying around of friends—just as we have seen happen here since the news of Brian's death.

It may be usual for the children to be present at the funeral of a parent. But it goes against the normal run of life for a parent to bury a child. So our hearts go out especially today to Brian's Mom and Dad. We pray that not alone will they have the consolation of a pride in a wonderful son and of a united family—which we all have witnessed over the past few days—but also the consolation of their faith, of knowing that Brian is now beyond all pain and suffering and has gone home to God our Father—to inherit the kingdom prepared for him—and for all of us—"since the foundation of the world."

There are a lot of young people here this morning, as there were last evening when Brian's funeral came to the church. For many of you, this will be your first experience of the death of someone in your *own* age group. You may even be closer to the altar today than you would be on an average Sunday. The speed of life does not usually allow you much time for long prayers or deep meditation. But today we are stopped in our tracks, trying to get our heads around the big questions, like: "What's it all about?" The second reading may point toward an answer: "We are always of good courage...for we walk by *faith,* not by sight."

Brian wasn't rich—but he left a legacy. In fact he left a *treasury,* a treasury of love. It seems that since he died that treasury has been opened. All of us around here have shared in it. We have experienced it in the coming together of friends, neighbors reaching out to each other, people wanting to help in any way they can, wonderful acts of kindness, the gospel of coming to life.

People in mourning often ask: "What can I do with all this love now that my friend has gone?" The best tribute, the best memorial, that we can make to Brian is to use that legacy of love. Giving it especially to those who need it most. "As long as you did it to one of these, the least of my brothers and sisters, you did it to me."

That's what the Lord wants of us and that's what Brian did. And we thank God for the sheer simplicity of his example of gospel living and giving in his young life. May he rest in peace.

Death of a Young Person

TO GRIEVE
WITH HOPE

Dick Lyng, O.S.A.

READINGS: WIS 4:7–15; ROM 8:14–18; MK 15:33–39

The Funeral Mass functions at many levels. We have gathered first of all to pray for Rory, that his soul may now find rest in God. We gather here also to offer our support to the Kavanagh family, to Rory's heartbroken parents, Des and Mary, to his brothers Ronan and Conal, to his girlfriend of five years, Colette. Through our presence here in such great numbers, we are stating publicly that we too recognize the blessing that Rory was. We are expressing gratitude to the Kavanagh family for molding Rory into that charming young man that he was, and for sharing him with the rest of us.

In the Funeral Mass too we strive to come to terms with reality, to face head-on the loss we have suffered, to peer into the heart of this dark mystery and to cry out in the words of the writer Joseph Conrad: "The horror, *The horror, The horror.*" The Funeral Mass should never be viewed as an escape from grief or a denial of death. Rather, the Funeral Mass teaches us to inhabit this darkness and to grieve with hope. The Kavanagh family will identify with that Calvary scene from Mark's gospel, and they will make their own the despairing cry of the dying Christ: "My God, My God, why have you abandoned us?"

But we will never come to terms with this grief unless we first savor the enormity of our loss. Even the loss of an elderly relative can be experienced as a cruel blow. The severing of old bonds can be painful. They are our own flesh and blood. With their death part of us dies. Pain seems to be the price that love demands. This is the law of life, the ordinary course of events. How much more painful then, how much more cruel, is the loss of a young life in tragic circumstances. The human reaction is one of numb disbelief. The Kavanagh family has been to hell and back several times since Sunday last. Their worst nightmare has conspired to overwhelm them. Their loss is acute only because they loved Rory dearly. An outgoing, vivacious, affectionate young man, he resisted the constraints of convention and location.

Rory was a wandering spirit, intellectually, artistically, and physically. He loved Italy. The spontaneity of the Mediterranean life appealed to him greatly. After completing his BA he dabbled professionally and successfully in the music business for a year. At the time of his death he was working in the computer business but, by all accounts, his ear and mind began to turn again to his first love, music. But, unfortunately, that dream remains unrealized. Rory would have understood perfectly the words of our first reading: "Length of days is not what makes age honorable, nor number of years the true measure of life." Life was a gift to be explored and celebrated. And, for him, the highest expression of that celebration was to be found in music.

Nine months ago, Rory was given a warning. A minor heart condition made him medically vulnerable. An alteration of lifestyle was called for. He was warned to cut back on his socializing and take regular exercise. He was scared by this warning, and he took it seriously for a time. But, as often happens, time deprived that warning of its original sting. The impatience of youth reasserted itself. Rory must have concluded that the safe, conventional life could best be lived by those who were good at it. His young life was snuffed out by that fatal flaw on Sunday morning last.

In the days and months ahead, Des and Mary, Ronan, Conal, and Colette will labor under a black cloud of grief. They will cling to treasured memories of Rory. As Des confessed, Rory inherited his good looks from Mary and his mischievous humor from Des. They will remember above all the affectionate center of a very close family, a beaming smile that lit up their lives. They will carry with them too some consoling memories from these dark days. They will treasure the outpouring of affection and grief from his great host of friends and peers. They will never forget that you stood shoulder to shoulder with them and held their hand as they stumbled blindly through this valley of darkness. To paraphrase the poet T.S. Eliot, "These fragments they have shored against their ruin." But their strongest support will come from their Christian faith, which I know has always been central to their lives and to the gentle way they live out their lives. They will draw strength from the knowledge that the God they worship has walked this dark path before them.

May Rory now find rest in God.

Death of a Young Person

THE SILENCE OF GOD

Richard Sheehy

READINGS: WIS 4:7–15; LK 24:13–35

When someone dies, we have a need to try to express what that person meant to us, what we feel they were about. Keara's friends and classmates have spoken very warmly and movingly of the young woman they knew. They have captured in little vignettes something of her rich personality.

When we highlight in retrospect what we admired in a person like Keara—her talents, her charm, her sense of purpose, her pursuit of excellence, her discipline, her sensitivity to others, her sense of fun, her independence of mind, her freedom of spirit, her depth, her beliefs—we are not trying to eulogize her beyond recognition. She would chide us for making her into a saint. Keara had her faults and weaknesses and would be the first to acknowledge them. She was not everybody's closest friend, but she was universally respected and admired. She was her own person.

But in recalling her qualities, we are, in fact, describing ideals

81

and values that we are attracted to and hold deep down—perhaps without even being aware of it. They are values that we consider important, goals that we are inwardly striving toward. We are touching into a deeper truth: that God gave us life, that our lives have purpose, and our task is to discover and pursue that purpose.

We want our lives to have meaning, to make a difference. We are not content to merely exist, to drift along enjoying life, to consume. Whatever our chosen branch of study or work here in college, most of us are not just in it to get a degree, or hopefully a job. We want to participate in the task of creating a more caring, compassionate, equitable, and open society, to make life more human for others; in effect, to realize the kingdom of God. St. Augustine said: "We were made for union with you; and our hearts are restless, until they rest in you." I know that Keara cared about other people—their aspirations and needs. It came through in her involvement in the college St. Vincent de Paul Society, particularly with the Sunday "hikes" for local children.

When Ignatius Loyola had to lie for months in a hospital bed, recovering from his war wounds, he used to dream about the great things he would do in the future, once he was well again (modeling himself on the lives of the saints he was reading about). It's good to dream, to imagine the world differently, but the future begins today, not tomorrow. More important than the things we plan to do in the future once we are qualified and have our degree, is allowing our dreams to shape the way we live now.

Keara had dreams, but she wasn't the kind to sit around waiting for things to happen. She pursued her goals and made personal sacrifices to make them happen, be it in the area of athletics, academic endeavor, or more personal achievements. As one of her friends remarked earlier, Keara wasted no time. She lived life fully, making the most of the present moment. The wise author of our first reading suggests that it's not how long we live that is significant, but rather *how* we live. What's important is not which gifts we have or don't have, but rather our willingness to develop and use the ones we do have.

So often we get caught up in the mundane tasks and deadlines of today that we lose sight of where we are heading. Keara's death stops us in our tracks and causes us to question again what is of ultimate value. We remember Keara today, not to be sad but to draw strength, comfort, and inspiration from all that she was and all that she packed into her short life. She would want us to encourage one another to embrace life as she did.

The disciples walking on the road to Emmaus thought that they were alone in their grief and could see only the tragic in what had taken place in Jerusalem. They wondered where God was—he seemed to have let them down. When Jesus walked with them and listened to their pain and loss, he helped them to gain a new perspective on all that had happened, and they realized that God was with them.

Keara's death, in the fullness of her youth and vitality and with so much ahead of her, is devastating. Michael and Gretta have lost a dear daughter; Fergal and Ronan, a beloved sister. We are at a loss to understand why such a freak accident should happen. We can feel let down, abandoned by God. However, another verse in the Book of Wisdom tells us: "Death was not God's doing, he takes no pleasure in the extinction of the living. To be—for this he created all."

Cardinal Martini, Archbishop of Milan, spoke of the silence of God in the face of human suffering. Sometimes silence is the only appropriate response to human tragedy, but it is silence charged with love and compassion. Good has already begun to emerge out of this experience of pain and loss. Keara's family has received much support from friends and neighbors and from Keara's classmates and friends. Students have been more sensitive to one another and have drawn closer together. The time, enthusiasm, and commitment that went into organizing today's memorial service speaks for itself.

My prayer is that the memory of how rich Keara's life was, of how deeply she touched the lives of so many people, and of how generous she was in death, may help bring healing, consolation, and pride to her family.

For Christians, the real meaning of death is revealed, not on Good Friday, but on Easter Sunday. I have a vivid memory of the day we said goodbye to Keara in Collooney—just as her coffin was being lowered into the ground, a bright sun appeared unexpectedly from behind dark November clouds and shone warmly on our faces. It seemed to point to another sun, the sun which rose on the morning of the Third Day.

Death of a Young Person

NOT MEASURED
BY YEARS

Benedict Hegarty, O.P.

READINGS: WIS 4:7–13; JN 11:17–27

This church has seen many funerals—all of them sad, some of them tragic. There is a special tragedy in the death of a young person. There is nothing we can say or think or do that can measure up to the loss of her family. This young person was in our midst. Like all young people she rejoiced in life, looked confidently to the years that lay ahead, dreamed of the way things might be. Now she is asleep. At a moment like this, the evident grief that clutches young and old alike testifies to a people's sense of loss and their loving support for this family.

There is only one prayer in the hearts of those who loved (name). There is only one question in their minds. Could we not have her back? Could these extraordinary and unbelievable days be wiped out? Could we awake from this nightmare? On two occasions, the gospels mention that Jesus wept. In both cases, it was the death of a young person—at the funeral of the widow's son and by the tomb of that young man Lazarus.

All we can offer, now, is a sense of shared loss, a touch of comfort, an assurance of love. Anything else we can do or say is sadly inadequate. Every death is tragic but the death of a young person touches a whole community. There is the loss of a young life; there is the well-up of sympathy within us for the family who mourn. There is a special sympathy—a special love, a special feeling—for the mother and father, the sisters, brothers, the close relatives and friends of (name).

The words of the first reading were penned by someone a long time ago, two thousand years ago and more. He wrote them, obviously trying to cope with a tragedy very like what we have seen over the past few days. He wrote these words helped by God for our comfort this morning. Remember them again. "The good person, though she die before her time, will find rest. For the age that is honorable comes not with the passing of time, nor can it be measured in terms of years. Young or old, it is understanding that is maturity; a good life this is fulfillment." We measure life so often by the number of years and its duration. Let's forget about numbers and length; let's think more of accomplishment. Think not of what (name) could have done or would have made of her life; think rather of all she had done and the light and love she left behind.

It was a short life she lived—but then what life is long? It is just that some lives are a little shorter than others. When we go out into the country and see the ruins of cottages and the marks of little fields, we might dream of those who lived there, who played, cared, loved, grew up, and died long hence. Life is very short for everyone.

Life is very short. However, a tragic death like this teaches us suddenly and painfully something deeply true. Life, too, is important. There would be no such sense of loss and grief unless we suddenly saw that life is very precious. When a life is torn away from us, then we see that our friends, people, life are all that matter.

We don't know why she had to go to Jesus so soon. A prayer in the liturgy to receive the remains has the words: "Now in his wisdom, he has called her to himself." We do not know what this wisdom is. We cannot trace its logic, its thoughts and purposes, and answer the question "why?" For us who believe, we only know that plan and wisdom is there and one day its truth will open to our uncomprehending eyes.

And it is not as if it has all ended. Her life has just taken a different shape and a different form. She and her family were deeply believing and they were so truly right. It is not as if they lost her; it is just that she is with them in a different way. A few days ago, God said: "(name), I have always loved you from the first moments of your life. Welcome home! You are no further from your mother and father and brothers and friends than I am, and I am so close to you all."

Death of a Young Person

IN THE LIGHT AND DARKNESS OF LIFE

Dermot A. Lane

READINGS: WIS 4:7–15; 2 COR 5:1–4; JN 11:17–21

The experience of death is always disturbing, but the death of a young person in the prime of life is overwhelming in its effects: it raises unanswerable questions, it challenges the very meaning and purpose of life, and it taxes our faith.

The sudden and tragic death of R. has stunned and shocked all of us gathered here this morning. In particular, the sudden departure of R. has created a deep void in the lives of G. and B., her parents, and in the life of K., her dear brother.

As we all know, R. was a unique and extraordinary young girl, full of life and vitality, gentle in her relationships with others, gifted with a great sense of humor, always sensitive and attentive to the needs of others. R. was someone who touched the lives of

88

others in so many different ways.

She was more than just a daughter to G. and B., she was also a friend and a companion. Likewise R. was more than just a sister to K., she was a trusted pal.

There is something inconsolable about parents having to bury a child. This sad experience is something that goes against the grain of nature and the rhythm of life itself.

In trying to come to grips with this untimely death of R., it is as well to acknowledge that there are no easy answers, that there is no cheap consolation in the face of death, that there are no satisfactory sound bites to soften the pain of loss. Pious platitudes ring hollow on occasions like these.

As we mourn the death of R. today, it must be said that it is a futile and empty exercise to speculate about what might have been if R. had not gone to Germany. What is much more important for us is to know that she was extremely happy during her last couple of weeks in Germany, that she wrote and phoned home regularly, sharing that happiness with her family. R. lived life to the full and died living life to the full and doing what she loved to do, namely horse riding and traveling and getting to know new people.

Likewise it is also a futile and empty spirituality that might blame God for this sad and tragic accident. It is not the will of God that R. should have been snatched prematurely from life in this disturbing way.

Instead, what is important for us is to realize that in these tragic circumstances God does not abandon us in our sadness and loneliness. On the contrary, God is with us both in the light and darkness of life, in the joys and sorrows, just as God was with Jesus in life and in death. This is the message that comes across in our readings that have been chosen by G. and B. and K. for this sad occasion.

In our first reading, we are reminded that it is not length of days that make a life honorable, but the way we have sought to please

God. R. sought to please God in her love of others.

Our second reading assures us that when the earthly tent we inhabit is destroyed, namely when this frail and fragile body that we live in is destroyed by accident or illness or age, then God will give us a new body, an everlasting home and dwelling place in heaven —an eternal home where one day we shall all be reunited "in Christ" when every tear shall be wiped away, and there shall be no more pain, no more mourning (Rev 21:1-5).

The foundation of our hope in this vision of life is given to us in our gospel reading in the words of Jesus: "I am the resurrection and the life. He who believes in me, though he die, yet shall he live and whoever lives and believes in me shall never die." These words of Jesus, addressed to Martha to console her over the death of Lazarus, are also addressed to us here today to console us in our loss of R. They assure us that death is not the end but the beginning of new life, that death is not a slipping away into nothingness but rather a re-creation unto eternal life with God. But most of all, these words of Jesus assure us that death is a gathering up of our personal life into God and a gathering into the assembly of God's people, into eternal communion with all who have gone before us through the power of the resurrection of Christ.

And so the sadness and loss of today gradually turns into a sense of gratitude for the life of R. With G. and B. and K., we thank God for the gift and grace of R., for the friendliness and cheerfulness that she shared with others, for the humor and warmth of her relationship with others.

And in the end we pray that each and every one of us, having loved R. here on earth, may continue to love her in eternity. Amen.

Death of a Child

INTO YOUR HANDS

Aidan Ryan

READINGS: LAM 3:17–26; MT 27:45–50

This church, over the years of its history, has seen many sad and tragic funerals. But few can have been as profoundly sad and sorrowful as the funeral that gathers us here today. The death of a child, in any circumstances, is an occasion of great sorrow. But a death that is the result of a freak and avoidable accident, simply beggars our understanding. While our lips pray the words of faith in the funeral liturgy, our hearts cry out in baffled bewilderment— what kind of a God could allow a young and innocent child to be snatched so cruelly from a loving and devoted family? Does he care? Is he there at all?

Well, I have no easy answers to these questions. All we can do is look at the figure of the crucified Christ and remember his words on the cross: "My God, my God, why have you forsaken me?" We can understand and identify with the desolate and despairing cry of the crucified Christ on the dark hill of Calvary.

91

Like him, we feel abandoned and forgotten by God in our pain and suffering. And yet the truth, the gospel truth, is that God had not abandoned him, and neither has he abandoned us. Jesus began to see the faintest glimmer of that truth in the final moments of his life as he prayed: "Father, into your hands I commend my spirit." The grace we seek from God here today is the grace to be able to make that prayer of Jesus our own as we commend our troubled and tortured spirits into God's loving hands. It takes a long time to travel the journey from "Why have you forsaken us?" to "Into your hands we commend our spirits." It's a journey that can't be rushed. For Joe's parents and his family, it may take years, it may take a lifetime. We are here as their neighbors and friends as they take their first painful steps along that road. We are here to stand with them in silent solidarity in the shadow of this immense cross.

In the opening prayer of this Mass, we prayed "though he was with us for so short a time, may he live, radiant and forever young in the kingdom of your love." Despite the darkness of this tragedy, our faith teaches us that the destination God has in store for Joe is just that—radiance and eternal youth in the kingdom of his love, where we can hope to see him again and be happy with him forever. For now, we continue to walk in the valley of tragic and untimely death. But we trust that Christ the Good Shepherd, who himself knew the darkness of Calvary, will in the end lead us into the bright joy of Easter morning, where every tear will be wiped away. On that day, we shall see you, our God, as you are, and be happy with you, and with Joe, forever in heaven.

Death of a Parent

A NEW KIND OF BELONGING

Niall Ahern

READING: JN 14:1–6

The death of a parent brings a new kind of unbelonging into a person's life. Before such a death, we were someone's son or daughter but now we are orphaned. Even an adult can be orphaned. To be without a parent is to be in a place of unbelonging.

And that's understandable. For one's parent is really one's first friend. One's longest first friend. No friend we will ever meet on life's journey will have been so interested or committed to us. No other friend will have known our first step or our first smile or our first tear. No other friend will know us through and through in such an intimate manner as to call us by our name—a name they themselves have chosen and given us. A parent is one who calls us by name for the first time.

Such uprootedness brings deep pain. We have to redefine

ourselves. We have to re-identify ourselves. Going from the place of being known through and through to a search for a new kind of identity is always painful. The loss is something we never get over. On this day of bidding farewell to a parent, there is a certain truth in saying we will never get over it. There is a certain truth in saying that life will never be the same again. And somehow we know in our heart's core that it is good to acknowledge that life will never be the same again; that there won't be the same kind of security; that there won't be the same depth of loving; that there won't be the same sureness of identity. One's parent and their loving of us are synonymous, and both have died today. So where, or to whom, do we now belong?

Someone once said to me that the only other word they could find for heaven was the word home. Homes are made in heaven but here on earth homes are built up by parents. They are the first creators of home. They create the safe place for us—the safe place to be born, to take initiative, to believe, to start the journey of loving. They are the heart of our home. Home, we all know, is where the heart is, and today the heart is not at home. The heart is gone from this place to a different space. For it is true that today home is joined to heaven in a more profound way. The one we love has gone before us to our eternal home. And it is our home too; the ultimate togetherness; where no separation or darkness or parting will ever happen again.

The parent who has just died has joined the host of heaven and remains part of the communion of saints, the family of God. Any apartness they may have experienced in life is now transformed beyond loneliness. We honestly are not sure what heaven is really like; it is beyond our imagining; it is our very best thought, our most carefully parceled gift, our longings all fulfilled. And so however sad and torn apart we are, we couldn't possibly want our parent back today. Maybe for our own sake—yes. But for their sake —no.

Go gently, dear Mum. Go gently to a rest beyond words. And may something of your new joy translate itself in time in our regard. We wait in eager longing and with one ray of hope amidst our running tears. And that ray shines out—hope. It brightens our darkness and guarantees our belonging with you always. That ray speaks to us in your name now and tells us how cherished we are by you forever. In your name it whispers: "Cherish everything of my care for you. Cherish my parenting of you, with all its fondest moments; its intimacy; its closeness. Cherish these and hand them on so that I might parent my children's children. Love is eternal and I'm here to welcome you to your eternal home. And so I say to you, my forever child, we will meet again on God's mountaintop in an embrace that will last forever. For together we belong and together we will be in the home of heaven. For this day brings for me, and for you, a new kind of belonging." Amen.

Death of a Parent

"WHEN THE SUN GOES DOWN"

Martin Delaney

READING: MT 5:13–16

It was one of those uniquely beautiful days that we sometimes get in late October or early November. Even though it was cold and crisp, the sun shone brightly for most of my long car journey from Kerry to Dublin. Evening was approaching as I entered the final phase of my journey, and I noticed that the magnificent sunshine that had been my loving companion on this day's journey was now about to leave me. Dusk descended quickly and then, in my rearview mirror, I noticed a curious object in the sky. At first I was not sure what it was, and then I realized it was the moon tentatively making its faintest appearance. Meanwhile my friend the sun, which had lit up so many of the faces I had seen on my journey that day, continued with its inevitable departure. However, my heart got a little lift when I noticed that, as the sun dipped lower in the sky, the moon behind me became brighter and brighter. When the sun finally disappeared, the moon majestically took its place as the brightest object in the sky.

During the final leg of my journey I reflected on the beautiful transition I had just witnessed. I realized that the moon was simply reflecting the light of the sun, now hidden from me. Somehow the moon was continuing the work of the sun. In some real way the moon assured me that the sun lived on eternally and continued to brighten up my life.

Today, as we say goodbye to N., a much loved mother, I am reminded again of that journey from Kerry to Dublin and the reflection I had as the sun went down only to be replaced by the different light of the moon. Like so many parents, N. lived her life like the sun. She brought light and warmth into the lives of her family. She was the source and sustainer of your lives. In the warmth of her embrace, all of you, her children and grandchildren, were empowered and enlightened. From your mother you received incredible gifts, and the energy to develop those gifts for the good of others. In her light was also reflected the light of her God, the love and compassion of God. *(The preacher could elaborate here a little on the particular life and gifts of the deceased.)*

Death of a Parent

STRUGGLING TO SEE

Michael Paul Gallagher, S.J.

READING: JN 14:1–6; 19–20

I last spoke to Kathleen on Thursday afternoon. I phoned her in the hospital to ask if I might visit. She was in great form because they had just told her she could go home for the weekend of her birthday. So we decided it was much better for me to visit her at home on Sunday. It would be, or would have been, her 59th birthday. But I never saw her again alive because, as we all know, Kathleen died in her own bed, in her sleep, that Saturday night. Sunday became her birthday in another sense, in the Christian sense of being born into a different life with God.

Today, of course, we think of her. Our minds are confused: I myself feel numb with sadness, and yet I remember so much that is good, happy, healing. We were childhood friends and have remained so all these years. We think of Kathleen, painfully because she is gone, but prayerfully and gratefully, because she lived a marvelously full and generous life as wife, mother, grandmother, and as nurse. But perhaps we think even more, in this church this morning, of Paul and of their three children. For such a happy family this is a huge loss, and we simply don't know what to say. But this overflowing church is itself a powerful word of sympathy, which means feeling pain with, sharing the suffering. To all Kathleen's family, our presence here in such numbers is like poetry without words. Because we have no real words worthy of how we feel, worthy of what we might want to say.

Over these short months after Kathleen discovered her illness, she did not have words either. Or else the words she found seldom did justice to her depth. I remember her total shock and anger at the beginning. Anger especially with God. In a friendly but tough way, she took it out on me a few times. "What kind of God would do this to me? I don't know if I believe anything anymore." And for weeks she wouldn't receive communion in the hospital when they came round in the early morning. And I had no easy answers. She even teased me about it. "You're meant to be an expert, and you've nothing to say to me." Then one day I said something utterly simple and without much thought behind it. I know it reached her because she repeated it to many of her visitors—and so it came back to me! I told her to forget about God and to remember only Jesus. It might sound heretical but, in fact, the word "God" has strange echoes of distance and power. But the person of Jesus rings so differently, not distance and power, but the opposite: closeness and weakness. Weakness with us. Especially in his own confusion and fear in the garden facing death.

Somehow that little sentence made a difference to Kathleen. She went back to receiving communion. And, these last weeks, panic seemed to give way to a kind of serenity. It was as if she was no longer fighting to win against death, only to lose generously, so to speak. She wanted to leave a sense of peace behind her. As if she wanted to nurse people into what she had discovered with such difficulty—a vision of goodness in spite of the darkness.

Forget about "God"—in quotation marks. Focus on Jesus Christ. In this spirit, let us turn again to those gospel words spoken by Jesus at his Last Supper, words intended to comfort his friends at the idea of his departure.

"Trust in me," he says, "I am the Way," and he adds, "the world will not see" but "you will see that I live." And then because of me, "you also will live." These simple words can offer us a poetry of hope, even within our numbness of these days. He is inviting us to see something that the merely human "world" cannot see. The life he spoke of lay beyond the darkness of his own death: it is the life that explodes for all of us with his resurrection. So Kathleen has not gone on her journey alone. And we pray to trust, in our darkness, what she now knows in her new light that Jesus is our Way: because of him she sees and lives; because of him we, too, in our different way, can see and live.

Death of a Parent

STILL WITH US

John Lyng, O.S.A.

READINGS: ACTS 10:34–36, 42; ROM 5:5–11; MT 5:1–12

In the course of the last thirty years, my mother wrote letters to me that included news of Funeral Masses in this church and the burials that followed. And, I suppose, for forty years before that, she wrote similar letters to her sister and brothers in places even farther away. They were the funerals of the fathers and mothers, the brothers and sisters, husbands, wives, and even children of most of you here today. Today, her turn has come. Sooner or later, it will be ours. And that, as we say, is the way with life.

When in prayer we remember the dead of any family, we remember the dead of all. And being human, we remember most sharply our own, those of our own house. Uppermost in some of your minds today are, no doubt, relatives of your own who died much younger and much more unexpectedly than our mother. The years are marks on our journey from birth to death. But they are like reversed milestones along the road; they only show us how far we have gone, not how far we have left to go. God decides that. So, some left early and some late. We pray for them all because they are important to us, and so we talk of them to our God. It's natural. They have all gone before us and, like ourselves, they are in need of God's mercy.

The ones that went before us left their mark on us; and that is putting it far too mildly. They didn't just mark us: they made us and shaped us and so are with us still. They are with us in the very shape of our bodies, in the way we walk or talk, in the things we enjoy and the things we fear, in the things we're good at and the things we couldn't do well in a fit; they're with us in the way we think, in the very way we blink our eyes or move our hands, our every tic and mannerism. They are part of ourselves and will always remain so.

We only seem to outlive our fathers and mothers. Even if they have gone ahead of us, they are still with us because they are in us. They refuse to go away. When we have to deal closely with death we are confused; we are upset; the familiar things of life are turned upside down. When we meet people who have lost someone close to them, we are glad to do anything we can to help. And that is good and necessary. But when it comes to what we feel, what we think, or what we should say about a death that is close to us, especially if that death is unexpected, we are uncomfortable or maybe even lost. When a child asks questions about the death of somebody it loves, it's hard to give satisfactory answers. And this is true no matter how strong or well-informed we are. Because death is the great proof of our weakness, the proof that we do not have all the answers, that the last word always lies with God, just as the first word was his too.

Death is a loss, a separation that we cannot avoid, and the parting is always sore. It is sometimes said that funerals can be joyful occasions, but I think that's a mistake. As we look to the salvation and eternal life of the one who has died, what mingles with the sadness of the mourning Christian is not joy, but hope. The second reading today tells us that our hope does not deceive us. It is founded on the one who died for us and defeated death for us. That is why Jesus could speak the strange words of today's gospel: "Blessed are those who mourn." The sadness of those who mourn is real sadness, but it does not blot out hope and expectation that where they have gone we will follow. We follow them to a place where all that is broken will be mended, all sickness cured, and happiness is found in what is true and good.

The mourning Christian is reminded of the highest joy, the resurrection, the defeat of death. When all hope and expectation for this life have melted away, when there is no longer any human answer, what awaits us is not the end but our Father. So, while death is a separation, it is also a homecoming. We believe this because we believe that Christ was raised from the dead. Paul says Christ's resurrection is a pledge to us, a guarantee from God, signed and sealed, that just as he raised Jesus he will raise us into his presence. The Christian faith does not help us to escape from death. It does not sweeten the bitterness of death. When we come to death we are at our very poorest. We come into this world with nothing. We leave in the same condition. Even if in the short years between our birth and our death we rule kingdoms and own millions. But Christ was there before us. He was at his poorest and weakest when he came to death. He was stripped of all respect and power, stripped even of his clothes. On the first Good Friday no resurrection was known. Isaiah's prophecy became a reality in him "Without beauty, without majesty we saw him, no looks to attract our eyes ... a man to make people cover their faces." Death is so often like that: something to make people cover their faces. We saw with our mother, and many of you saw with your own, someone who was a pillar of strength in mind and body become weak and helpless, confused and broken. This is hard to take. But resurrection faith assures us that, at the final point of human weakness and defeat, at the moment when we are brought to nothing, we meet God and are raised by him.

Each of us is a tenant. Anything we have in this life has been given to us on trust by God. We hold only temporary possession. We are each given a small part of God's farm or vineyard to cultivate. Of course, we don't all get the same quality plot of land. Some of us get the rich land of good health, good fortune, kind friends, and high abilities, while others get the hard ground of poverty, misfortune, and maybe unjust treatment. But we can be sure of this: our landlord, God, makes merciful allowance for these differences when we go to pay the rent.

As we talk and think about men and women who have come to the end of their strength, we would be poor Christians indeed if we forget those who do the hard and silent work of taking care of them. Some names come to my mind and others will come to yours.

My mother, and all the others we remember today, have gone round the corner ahead of us, and the manner of their going is no longer relevant. What does matter is that while here, they, in their different ways, showed us some of the goodness that God puts into men and women. It was, largely, through them that God has been good to us. So, we give thanks to God for their lives, and it is with confidence that we pray to the same God to give them eternal rest.

Death of a Single Person

THE SOULS
OF THE VIRTUOUS

Aidan Ryan

READINGS: WIS 3:1–6, 9; MT 5:1–12

Those of you who attend funerals frequently will be very familiar with today's first reading. It is probably the most frequently used reading of all at Funeral Masses. It could even become so familiar that we no longer hear what it is saying. So today, as we give back into the hands of God the soul of Mary Byrne, I suggest that we look more closely at it.

It is from a part of the Old Testament called the Book of Wisdom. Now, wisdom is a very rich word in the Scriptures. It indicates something much deeper than intelligence or cleverness. Wisdom is having a sense of what is really important in life, and what is secondary or less important. It is the ability to discern what is of lasting value and what is of passing concern. It is a capacity to see things in the light of eternity and from God's point of view. Mary Byrne was a person who had something of all this in her approach to life, so it is especially appropriate that we should read from the Book of Wisdom at her funeral. So let me pick just three sentences from the first reading, sentences that throw light on the mystery of death in a general way, and today, for us, suggest ways of looking at the death of Mary Byrne.

The first sentence in the reading says "the souls of the virtuous are in the hands of God." Mary was a good living person all her life and now her soul is in God's hands—the loving, welcoming, warm hands of her creator. In what better or safer place could she be?

Then the line "slight was their affliction, great will their blessings be"—Mary had her share of loneliness and sorrow and her share of pain in her final illness. But all of that is over now, and it pales into insignificance in the blessed happiness and joy of the vision of God in heaven.

Then the last line: "grace and mercy await those he has chosen." Many years ago, God chose Mary in baptism to be his beloved child, on whom his favor would always rest. Now he welcomes her with his grace, which is the gift of his free and unconditional love, and his mercy, which is his compassionate understanding of human weakness and sinfulness, and his readiness and eagerness to forgive and to welcome us, just as we are in our imperfections and limitations.

So as we escort Mary by our prayers toward her final destination in heaven, we thank God for his constant presence with her in life and in death. We pray for the wisdom to understand something of what God has prepared for those who love him, or even try to love him. We commend the gentle and virtuous soul of Mary into his loving hands.

Tragic Death

WAITING BEYOND WORDS

Niall Ahern

READING: MK 15:33–39

Silence is really the only response to death, but when death happens tragically even the silence is inadequate. In the Book of Lamentations we are told that it is good to wait in silence for the Lord to save, and that is really all we can do when death strikes tragically. Wait. All we can do is wait.

We have to wait on God because in tragedy God seems absent. What he has allowed to happen is so violent, is so corrupt, is so unnatural—that we can only wait to see if he can make any sense of the event that makes no sense to us.

The question is always—Why? Why can a good God allow such terrible sadness to enter into a person's life? The tragedy could have been avoided. There were so many circumstances that could have gone the other way. Why did he let it happen to me—to my family—to my community? We have to wait on words to form any answer.

And here words are always small. Tragedy has no place for small words of comfort, and even the gospel words of God's love and care and tenderness seem a parody of whom he truly is. Like the people in the crowd in Elie Wiesel's book *Night* who cried out as the young boy hung dying on the gibbet, "Where is your God now?"—the question always in tragedy is, "Where is God now?' And the answer comes back to us as it did to them, "He is here— he is hanging on the tree."

God is in tragedy. The God we believe in always inhabits our sadness. He always desires to be at the center of those events in our lives that we cannot understand ourselves. A tragic death, more than any other event, causes us to live the mystery of faith. Tragedy proclaims the mystery of faith. That's what we say at Mass—Christ has died, Christ is risen, Christ will come again. There is no understanding tragedy except within the mystery of faith. Such mystery goes beyond words.

Tragic death faces us with the mystery of life itself—not with circumstances of birth or with length of days or with conditions of living or even with the moment of dying. The mystery is that life was given to us at all. And it is the quality of our living, rather than the detail of our dying, which is of most significance. William Blake tells us:

We are put on this earth a small space
that we might learn to bear the beams of love.

That's the focus to which we are invited today. Not the horror of death's visitation, but rather the beams of love. The harrowing of this moment cannot—dare not—obliterate the love that inhabited this life; a life cut down by a kind of wayward carelessness, but a life we celebrate today. And we celebrate silently because words of love are most poignantly articulated in the heart and not in the head.

The horror of today somehow invites us to celebrate all that was loving and lovely and tender and worth cherishing in the midst of this unexpected and intrusive death. Each one here knows and experienced something of the love sent out by the one we mourn, and no act of love sent out into the abyss of time comes back unclaimed or unheralded.

Let us claim and herald all that was good and noble and pure in this life, so suddenly physically terminated. We will not be overcome by the tragedy alone—but rather will be possessed by the life that was larger than death. This life of love was shared with us. And may it be so eternally.

And what harm if we stand in embarrassed silence or wait in a togetherness beyond definition? The disclosure of the mystery of God requires waiting. To know that we stand together in some way authentically and real—we must wait beyond words. But God is in the waiting and speaks love in our hearts. The one who has been wrenched from us was God waiting in love for us. The love we knew has returned to the love that made it. Why did this happen now? Why at all? We don't know. But with Thornton Wilder we do know:

> ... we ourselves shall be loved for a while and forgotten. But that love will have been enough. All our impulses of love return to the love that made them. Even memory is not necessary for love. There is a land of the living and a land of the dead and the bridge is love—the only survival, the only meaning.

Tragic Death

SUSPENDED IN DISBELIEF

John Littleton

READINGS: WIS 3:1–6, 9; PS 115; LK 12:35–40

Tragedy always stuns us. This is especially true when we experience the tragic and sudden death of someone we love dearly. We are shocked as individuals and we are visibly shaken as a community when we learn about the unexpected and premature death of someone we have known so well. We are numbed by the suddenness and the horror of it. We cannot understand it. We have so many questions, and we have no answers. We have no satisfactory explanations. We do not want to believe or accept that the person we have known so well and loved so much is dead. In a sense, we are paralyzed. We are suspended in disbelief.

Today there is a huge emptiness in our hearts because Margaret, whom we have known and loved, has been taken from us. It is so unfair and so cruel that she has been taken away from us in this way. Margaret was so young and full of life. Her work in this world was not finished. She was in the prime of her life and she was healthy. She still had so much to do and so much to give to other people. We are tempted to say that if she had been elderly—and her death had not been so sudden and tragic—we could accept it. We would be sad, of course, but we could accept her death in such circumstances. It is no wonder, then, that we are devastated at this time. Our grief is enormous. What are we to do? How are we to cope?

Today, we need more than ever to listen attentively to the message of the word of God. Only our faith in God can sustain us and prevent us from remaining suspended in disbelief as we mourn Margaret's death and struggle to cope with our sense of loss. Only the word of God can offer us consolation and hope when we are confronted with the frailty and uncertainty of human life.

Everyone here today can identify so easily with what has been read to us in the first reading from the Book of Wisdom: "their going looked like a disaster, their leaving us like annihilation." These words certainly apply to Margaret's untimely death. However, we must also listen to the reassurance, concerning Margaret and many other people who have died, offered to us through the word of God in the Book of Wisdom: "but they are in peace ... those who are faithful will live with him in love; for grace and mercy await those he has chosen." Our faith in the risen Christ encourages us to hope that Margaret is now in peace and enjoying eternal life. We pray that, through God's mercy and forgiveness, Margaret has made her own the words of the response to the psalm: "I will walk in the presence of the Lord in the land of the living." Even so, we will continue to pray for her and ask her to pray for us.

But what about us who remain behind? What about us who gather here around Margaret's dead body and, in particular,

Margaret's family members who are heartbroken? The word of
God, in addition to reassuring us about Margaret, has a relevant
and compelling message for us, too—a message that, if we listen
to it and act accordingly, will ensure that we will be ready for
death whenever it comes, whether suddenly in tragic
circumstances or slowly at the end of a terminal illness or in old
age. In the gospel reading from Luke, which was read to us, Jesus
says: "You too must stand ready, because the Son of Man is
coming at an hour you do not expect." Strange words, perhaps,
but true words. None of us knows when our life in this world will
end. How many of us are ready for death at this moment? The
only meaningful way to be ready for death is to prepare
purposefully by loving God and all God's people in everything we
do.

So there is a definite lesson for us to learn during these
sorrowful and lonely days. The lesson is to begin to learn not to
be surprised by surprises, or the suddenness of the unexpected.
Life and death are mysterious and, therefore, full of surprises.
Some of these surprises are remarkably rewarding and happy;
others are disturbing in their sadness. We need to prepare for the
unexpected. We will never be unprepared if we use properly the
various opportunities and possibilities given to us in life. We need
to celebrate life and live it fully while we have it. Then, when
tragedy happens, indeed we will be shocked and stunned. But we
will not remain suspended in disbelief for too long because, even
in our grief, our Catholic faith will enable us to continue to live in
hope until we meet God in death.

"JESUS WALKS WITH US IN OUR SUFFERING"

Martin Delaney

READING: LK 24:35–48

I'm standing here this morning before this great gathering of people brought together by the common bond of the tragic death of a young person we all knew. I am very much aware that all words are inadequate to temper our grief or to begin to heal the pain being so keenly felt in this church this morning. And yet we have to talk, as we have been talking over the last few days. Since John died we have all been telling stories, asking questions, and getting no answers. We all want to know why this had to happen. Was there something we could have done? Why? Why? Why? For so many people in this church today, the death of John last Thursday has turned their world upside down. We have all been plunged into a great darkness, and we are desperately looking for a little light.

I presume that no one here this morning is unaware that John took his own life. I believe it is important that we acknowledge it publicly, to hear those words spoken aloud, and not just whisper them privately among ourselves. In this way we can try to deal with it. We can perhaps begin to acknowledge that, in addition to the terrible loss and grief that comes with the sudden and tragic death of someone so young, there may also be feelings of anger within our hearts. Anger with John, anger with society, anger with ourselves. We will probably never know why this tragedy happened, but what we do know is that John was greatly loved by many people, particularly by his parents, Maureen and Jimmy, and by his brothers and sisters. John also loved them and a great many other people too, and somehow in his troubled heart John believed that what he was doing was out of love for those in his life. This is very difficult for us to understand but it may be some consolation to know that just as John had brought so much love to others in life, he also believed that his death was a loving act too, that somehow he was lifting a burden from your shoulders.

But for you, Maureen and Jimmy, and for all of you who loved John so much, I know that this death has brought you a great burden of sorrow and pain. I would like to share something with you that I hope will make some sense to you. Every year I visit many primary schools around the diocese, and I am always amazed by the variety of questions about religion that the children have. However, there is one question that I am asked more than any other: Why is Good Friday called *Good?* How could the cruelty of the crucifixion ever be seen as good? In asking this question, the children are focusing in on one of the ageless mysteries of our Christian faith. Why did Jesus have to suffer on Calvary? Why could he not have climbed down from the cross triumphantly? Surely the Roman soldiers and the Centurion would have dropped to their knees in homage, and the people of Jerusalem, who only a few short hours earlier had demanded his death, would have rushed up the hill to worship him. The whole world would soon have known that certainly Jesus Christ was the Son of God.

But this did not happen. It did not happen because, as Jesus told the two disciples on the road to Emmaus and again reminds the frightened gathering in the upper room of today's gospel: It was necessary that the Christ should suffer these things. The Scriptures for centuries had been foretelling this very truth. Necessary, not by some abstract truth or law of nature, but because this was the way God wanted it. This was the way God wanted it, and Jesus in free obedience accepted this charge from his Father. But it was precisely through this emptying of himself, through his acceptance of suffering and death, that he won victory over death.

But why? Why a blood-soaked death when surely there were other ways open to an all powerful, all knowing God? Why a death so horrific that Jesus himself asked to be spared of it at the eleventh hour? The honest answer is that we really do not know. We get some clue from Jesus himself when he talks of his suffering and death as being rooted in God's love for each of us: "Greater love than this no man has, than he lay down his life for his friends" (Jn 15:13). Somehow, by rising from the dead and conquering suffering and pain, after he had fully entered into the darkness and despair which that very suffering and pain brought him, Jesus could powerfully identify and empathize with our struggle and pain. And not only could he identify with our suffering and pain, but he could show us a way through it, give it a purpose.

If Jesus had triumphantly climbed down from the cross and escaped all the human suffering that went with it, would he have anything to say to John's heartbroken family and friends today? I think not. As it is, the only real source of hope and healing for this gathering this morning is that somehow our suffering and pain today is intimately linked with the suffering and death of Jesus Christ, the Son of God. But just as our suffering and pain, and

John's suffering and pain and death, are linked with Jesus, so too the resurrection of Jesus allows us all the exact same hope. "So you see how it was written that the Christ would suffer and on the third day rise from the dead" (Lk 24:47).

Note: In cases of a tragic death like this, the preacher should discuss the content of the homily with the bereaved family beforehand.

Tragic Death—by Suicide

DE PROFUNDIS

John Wall

READINGS: EZEK 34:11–12; 15–16; PS 130;
ROM 8:14–18; JN 11:17–27

"If only…." These are words we often use, but especially when we experience tragedy or great stress—like the sadness all of us experienced at the shocking news of this tragic passing of Stephen. And we find exactly the same sentiment expressed by Mary in the gospel today. She says to Jesus *"if only* you were here" this would not have happened. It's a natural reaction.

I remember when I was a student in the seminary, a very wise and experienced teacher on the staff told us: "When you meet a situation of extreme frustration, as all tragedies are, you will find two strong emotions—blame and guilt. Both are natural but neither is helpful. They are just expressions of the anger of frustration."

The frustration is felt because Stephen was much loved—loved by his parents, family, and many friends. If care could have kept him, he would still be with us.

117

Stephen was a fine young man, enthusiastic in his generosity. He was also a very sensitive person, perhaps too sensitive for his own good. In his sensitivity he felt things deeply. And that same sensitivity that gave him a sympathy and a thoughtfulness for others, caused him to feel the pain of life more keenly than others might feel it.

Drugs were taken initially as an anaesthetic against the pain of life and because they were readily available—and then continued because of the entrapment of addiction that he so bravely tried to overcome. And we know that it was his frustration with that addiction that led to the tragedy of his death.

We leave all judgment to God, with whom "there is mercy and fullness of redemption." In the funeral prayers we pray that God will "forgive any sin we committed through the frailty of our human nature." We also recall that "God remembers the good that we have done and forgives our sins." In that Spirit we pray today for Stephen, remembering the words of Jesus from the cross: "Father, forgive them, for they know not what they do."

And we pray too that those who loved Stephen dearly will be able to forgive and let go of any anger they may feel from the frustration of his passing.

In our second reading, St. Paul is prompted by the Spirit to cry out: "Abba, Father" in prayer to God—surely the God of Ezekiel in our first reading, who will search for his sheep "and will rescue them from all places where they have been scattered, on a day of clouds and thick darkness." Surely, he will bring Stephen safely home.

We cry out too to the Christ of our gospel today, the Christ of our frustrations. The Christ who was approached by Mary in *her* frustration at the death of her brother. The Christ who wept for his friend Lazarus.

We know, as Mary did, that all *will* be well, that Jesus is the resurrection and the life. But what do we do in the meantime?

There are a lot of people out there, hurting and in need of our help. There is a lot to be done in the battle against drugs. We pray for that gift, to work out our frustrations by practical caring and following the example of Jesus in the gospel. In that way Stephen's death will not be in vain, but rather it can become an occasion to spur us on to look after those who really need us.

Death after a Long Illness

LIFE IS CHANGED, NOT ENDED

John Littleton

READING: MK 15:33–39

Today is a sad and lonely day. At last, Michael, a husband, a father, a neighbor, and a friend to many people, has died. He has gone from this life. But, in a sense, today is also a day of relief, particularly for his wife and children who sat at his bedside and watched him dying slowly and, until the last few days, painfully. Now he suffers no more pain. He is no longer distressed. He no longer struggles to die. He is finally in peace, and we are grateful for this.

Sometimes it seems that God has deserted us. When most people, including Michael, discover that they are terminally ill, they are usually frightened, and they plead with God, asking him to restore them to health. They may become angry with God when, having asked for his help, he seems to do nothing; at least, God does not respond in the way they would wish. This is especially true regarding the pain and the distress associated with serious and terminal illness. Their faith in God's goodness and care is challenged and tested. Like Jesus dying on the cross, they may cry: "My God, my God, why have you deserted me?"

Then there are family members, neighbors, and friends, who watch helplessly and in anguish as someone they love gradually wastes away and dies. We pray that God will intervene in some miraculous manner and make him better. We may even begin to bargain with God in the vain hope that our bargaining will make a difference. But, in the end, the person we love dies and there is nothing we can do about it. Again, like Jesus dying on the cross, we may also cry: "My God, my God, why have you deserted me?"

Today, as we gather in church at Michael's funeral, in the midst of our grief and sadness we are professing our Christian faith in the resurrection of the dead and eternal life. We are affirming our belief— although it does not always seem reasonable—that, while all life on this earth is terminal and while death is a fact of life, death is not the end for Michael or, indeed, for any of us. There is life after death: life that never ends. Even in our sadness, we believe that Michael's death in this life has been his birth into eternal life. Michael lived to die and, ironically, he died to live. This is the real mystery of life and death. Therefore Michael's life is changed, not ended. It is our prayer that Michael is now enjoying eternal life with God.

Michael experienced much suffering toward the end of his earthly life. But, in our hearts, we know that suffering can have great value— no matter how incomprehensible this may seem to us today. Through pain and suffering we learn what it means to embrace the cross of Christ. Like Jesus, dying on the cross, our faith is tested when we experience suffering, and when we witness suffering in other people's lives. And just as God did not desert Jesus, he does not desert us, and did not desert Michael. It is our hope that Michael's suffering has not been in vain but, instead, has prepared him to live a life that has changed, not ended, and to rest in God's peace and love forever.

Death after a Long Illness

GRATITUDE in GRIEF

Ambrose Tinsley, O.S.B.

READING: LK 23:44–46

(The following homily was given, not with the funeral Mass, but on the previous evening when the body had been taken to the church.)

This passage that we have just heard continues by recording the reaction of the soldier who was standing by the cross. He praised God, we are told, proclaiming that the one who died was certainly a person who was good and great. Tonight, as we now pay our last respects to Joan, I feel that that same kind of tribute should be paid to her as well. That may sound almost trite, like some of those remarks that people make without reflection when a person whom they knew has died. But, even if it does, that doesn't mean that it cannot be true. The Joan whom I knew in her final years was certainly both good and great, and I do not have any doubt at all that her considerate and gentle presence will be sorely missed.

Our sympathies, of course, go in a special way to John her

husband, to Helena and Siobhán, to Joan's own parents who were able to come down to see her some few days ago. Indeed our sympathies to all who have been shocked by what may have appeared to some to have been quite a sudden, unexpected death.

But Joan had no illusions. After her mastectomy, she had prayed for the gift of three more years. And God was good. He granted her request. She then not only did all that she could for her own family, but started visiting the patients in a nearby hospice too. In that way she repeatedly and with courage faced the dark reality of that disease that also threatened her. The next stage in her journey, which I have been able to identify, took place last summer when she was at home. There, in the sunshine of her garden, she experienced within herself a feeling that the end for her was not too far away. It was a premonition which, just two months later, turned to physical concern.

One reason why I chose this section of the passion story for the gospel of tonight is that it manifests for us the mind of Christ when he was faced with his approaching death. "Into your hands I commend my spirit," he exclaimed. Joan never used those words, at least to me, but her acceptance of what was to happen was complete. Indeed, it seemed at times so total that I felt within myself a certain sense of awe. There seemed to be in her a secret and a sacred depth that gave her strength to face and to accept what was to come. And when it did, she very quietly gave her own spirit to the One in whom she had put all her trust.

The other reason why I chose this gospel passage is because of that short phrase: "The veil of the temple was torn in two." Its implication seems to be that people then began to see what had been veiled from them before. For instance, through the death of Christ they recognized in him a goodness that they realized had come from God and, as they later contemplated it, their lives were obviously changed. Indeed, as we have heard, the soldier at the cross perceived a goodness in the one who died and found that, consequently, he was able to give praise to him from whom all goodness comes. Is it too soon for us to do the same? Is it too soon to give God thanks and praise for all the goodness that he has revealed to us through Joan? I know we grieve, how could we not, but I at least find consolation in the words of Jerome, that great human saint who, writing to a friend whose mother had just died, declared, "we thank God that we had her for so long." If our own mood today is one of grieving at the loss of someone whom we loved, there surely is a level in our hearts where we are grateful to have known her and to have experienced her goodness in our lives.

It is a pity that this note of gratitude is not expressed explicitly in the funeral rite itself. However, when we gather here tomorrow morning it will be to celebrate the Eucharist which is, as its name implies, a service of thanksgiving. Then, despite our grief, we will be asked to give thanks to the Lord our God for all the many blessings that we have received and, consequently, for the ones that came to us through Joan. Perhaps, at such a moment, we will even be aware that she is somehow with us still. If not, that day will surely come, and then our gratitude for all that she has done for us, and can do still, will consequently grow.

Death of an Autistic Youth

GENIUS AND HANDICAP

Eltin Griffin, O. Carm.

READING: LK 10:21-23

They say that the presence of a genius in the home can have as great an effect on the equilibrium of a family as that of a disabled child. But when genius and disability are combined in the one child, the challenge seems insuperable. And yet none of us would have been without Paul. His Adonis-like face and figure, his utterly beautiful countenance, his enormous height, his prodigious strength, his intellectual grasp of disparate and disconnected areas of knowledge—these are aspects of Paul we will always remember, recall, recount, and retell. There were times when he made incredible demands on his family, on his parents, on his brothers and sisters, on relations and friends, times when he upset the entire household, when he threw it into disorder and confusion—but through his bizarre, strange, and amusing ways he made a distinct and distinctive contribution to the life of the family, brought out in each and all of them undreamt of depths of strength, dedication, and love. Paul was the glue in his family even when he became too much for them to handle any longer and had to be put into special care. He left a void behind him, a place in the household that could never be filled.

Paul, in normal circumstances, would have been an undoubted genius, in the area maybe of higher mathematics or of music. He might have excelled his parents in artistic expression. Why should such expression have been denied him? Is it fair that such genius should be trammelled, should be prevented from expressing itself, leading to extraordinary tantrums and frustration?

I can't claim to have all the answers. I cannot act the part of God except to say that in life we are all trammelled—we are all hindered—we are all prevented through circumstances from giving total expression to all our gifts, no matter how comfortably we may try to arrange our lives. We suffer from the limitations of time and space, from the limitations imposed on us by lack of finance, lack of time, lack of understanding by other people (even those who are close to us), lack of support when it is needed. Our efforts never reach the total degree of perfection we might desire. Limitation is part of life. Many an artist, on seeing or hearing the end product, has been forced to say "That is not what I meant at all," even though others may hail it as a masterpiece.

It is only in another life that we can let go of limitation, as we enter into a transcendental relationship with the universe, with the whole of creation, with the Heavenly City, and with the Master and Lord of the universe, who draws us all into total communion with all that exists and to the transformation of our beings.

For Paul, limitation has given way to limitless possession, to that fulfillment for which his whole being cried out. And so, at the request of Frances, we give thanks to God, as we have done in the gospel this morning, in the words of Mary in the Magnificat.

People will say it is a merciful release. Easy to say, but there is still the pain of letting go. Life is full of letting go. Parents are forever letting go. It is in the numerous letting goes that parents attain their full maturity. They are no longer needed, the prelude may be for the final letting go.

Books, plays, and novels have been written on this familiar theme. C. Day Lewis says, in his attractive poem on the subject, "Love is proved in the letting go."

AN UNBELIEVER

Michael Paul Gallagher, S.J.

READING: MT 25:31–40

We may know that parable of the Last Judgment too well, and so we miss its shock effect. If I try to translate it into more modern language, it is saying, surprisingly, that faith is not on the final examination paper. But love is. Indeed, it is the only topic being examined, because it is God's way of measuring our lives. As St. John of the Cross put it, with a certain play of words, "in the evening of life we will be judged by love." By the love we lived. And by the Love, capital L, who is God. That parable, then, contains a happy surprise for those who are not sure of God. They are like those people in the judgment story who ask: "but where did we ever know you?" "As often as you did it to one of these least of mine, you did so to me."

Many of you here this morning will realize why this gospel is so fitting for the funeral of our friend Eamon. He was not a church-goer and, indeed, some years ago I remember his talking to me about what he called his "block about God." He didn't like the labels "atheist" or "non-believer." Indeed he liked to joke that he believed too much. He believed people, especially if they told him they needed his help in some way—from beggars on the street to those in drug rehabilitation to whom he devoted most of his working life. He believed in his work as making a difference, even when it was tough going or when failures left him angry or hurt.

Perhaps because Eamon encountered so much pain in people, he found it all the harder to believe in God. Is that not true of all of us when we run into the desolations of life? But which God becomes incredible in those darker times? Possibly the God who seems beyond all struggle, the God who is meant to control everything and lets so much tragedy happen. We heard one surprise in the gospel—that love is the measure, that faith is, in a strange sense, secondary.

There is another surprise imaged in front of us above the altar, an image we become so used to seeing that it too loses its shock. On the cross we see a man dying, and we dare to believe that he is dying because of love, because of love for us, and that he is also God among us. The crucifix puts an end to all those pagan images of a God beyond struggle or pain. I wonder, or at least I dare to wonder, whether Eamon ever really had the chance to ponder who this God is, this Crucified One who loved, and suffered because he loved. In prayer for Eamon this morning, we ask that his loving and his suffering carry him to the surprise of Christ's gratitude: "whenever you cared for all those wounded ones that came your way, you were meeting me."

A final reflection, more for us who live on than for Eamon who has left this place of searching. If love is the measure, then what difference does faith make? Eamon loved stories. I answer with a story to explore this question about "why faith, if love is the key?" Once upon a time, there was a queen who asked one of her close friends to carry a bag for her from one village to another. The bag was heavy but the friend carried it because he was asked to do so and because the queen was his friend. When he came back, the queen asked him, "What did you think was in that bag?" "I wondered about it but have no idea," he answered. "Suppose it was rubbish in the bag," said the queen, "would that upset you?" "It might," replied the friend, "but not all that much: I was carrying it because you asked me to." "Yes, you carried it without knowing," said the queen, "but if you had known there was pure gold in the bag, it would have made a difference."

We are asked to carry life with love. We are also invited to know the pure gold of faith. Eamon carried much, and if he sometimes imagined the gold, perhaps he thought that was too good to be true. On the other side of death he now knows in a way that we cannot, but we can pray that Eamon enjoy that surprising welcome of Christ.

THE CONTRIBUTORS

Niall Ahern is Administrator of St Mary's Cathedral, Sligo.

Martin Delaney, parish of St John, Kilkenny, is Diocesan Advisor for
Religious Education in the diocese of Ossory.

Michael Paul Gallagher, S.J. is a writer and teacher.

Eltin Griffin, O. Carm. is a liturgist, writer, and preacher.

Benedict Hegarty, O.P. is a scripture scholar and Prior of St
Saviour's, Dublin.

Dermot A. Lane, theologian and writer, is parish priest of Balally,
Dublin.

John Littleton is a theologian and curate in the parish of Doon,
County Limerick.

Dick Lyng, O.S.A. is parish priest of St Augustine's, Galway.

John Lyng, O.S.A. is an Augustinian missionary in Maiduguri,
Nigeria.

Brendan McConvery, C.Ss.R. is a scripture scholar and preacher.

Brian McKay, O. Carm. is a formation director and retreat guide.

Betty Maher is a writer whose latest book is *Called to be a Nuisance:
Reflections from the Fringe*.

Lawrence E. Mick, a priest of the Archdiocese of Cincinnati, is
engaged in a ministry of liturgical formation and parish renewal.

Aidan Ryan is parish priest of Carrickedmond, County Longford.

Richard Sheehy is a chaplain at Trinity College, Dublin.

Ambrose Tinsley, O.S.B. is a monk of Glenstal Abbey.

John Wall is parish priest of Seville Place Parish, Dublin.

Thomas R. Whelan C.S.Sp., liturgist, is Director of Studies at the
Kimmage Mission Institute, Dublin.